FEEL THESE WORDS

Feel These Words

WRITING IN THE LIVES OF URBAN YOUTH

Susan Weinstein

Published by
State University of New York Press, Albany

Cover photo by Guillermo Delgado.

For information, contact State University of New York Press, Albany, NY
www.sunypress.edu

Production by Diane Ganeles
Marketing by Michael Campochiaro

Library of Congress Cataloging in Publication Data

Weinstein, Susan, 1965-
Feel these words : writing in the lives of urban youth / Susan
Weinstein.
    p. cm.
Includes bibliographical references and index.
ISBN 978-1-4384-2651-8 (hardcover : alk. paper) —
ISBN 978-1-4384-2652-5 (pbk. : alk. paper)
1. Creative writing (Secondary education)—Illinois—Chicago—Case
studies. 2. English language—Composition and exercises—Study and
teaching (Secondary)—Illinois—Chicago—Case studies. 3. Youth—
Education (Secondary)—Illinois—Chicago—Case studies. I. Title.
LB1631.W354 2009
808'.066071277311—dc22
                                                    2008033402

10 9 8 7 6 5 4 3 2 1

To my students

Contents

Acknowledgments

There are too many people to thank, and I'm sure I'll forget someone. So, with apologies to the inadvertently excluded:

Without Todd DeStigter, I may never have embarked on a PhD; without Dave Schaafsma, I surely wouldn't have had the quality of graduate experience that I did. These two professors guided me through my doctoral program at the University of Illinois at Chicago and made me the envy of other graduate students who didn't have the unwavering support that these two gave (and continue to give) me. They are my models for working with my own graduate students, and I simply cannot thank them enough.

Several other professors at the University of Illinois at Chicago were central to my professional development. Bill Ayers, Ralph Cintron, and Jamie Daniel served as generous teachers and insightful critics as members of my dissertation committee; in two graduate seminars, I benefited from Marcia Farr's years of ethnographic experience. My peers at UIC—including Annie Knepler, Naomi Crummey, and Jennifer Cohen—provided much-needed intellectual and social support. My fellow assistant directors at the UIC Writing Center—Eva Bednar, Candace Rai, Carrie Brecke, and Margaret Gonzales, among others—made my stint there an unmitigated pleasure, while the director of the Writing Center, Vainis Alexis, may always be the most dedicated, positive, selfless (and underappreciated) professional I've ever known.

My teaching colleagues and students at *La Juventud* Alternative High School taught me so very much, and words honestly fail me in attempting to describe the intensity of that experience. Suffice it to say that *La Juventud* is the place where I began to understand exactly how much young people can withstand and still get up every morning (sometimes late, but still . . .) to try to learn and make lives for themselves.

The English Department at Louisiana State University made my transition from dissertator to assistant professor smoother than I had any right to expect. Special thanks go to Lisi Oliver, my fabulous faculty mentor, and to Brannon Costello and Pallavi Rastogi, who have provided feedback of incalculable worth regarding this book. Other LSU colleagues who read and commented on the book include Laura Mullen, Jackie Bach, and Robert Hamm.

I have been lucky to find friends in Baton Rouge who have led me seamlessly into my new research on teen spoken word poetry; the remarkable Anna West(siiiiiide!) and Chancelier xero Skidmore are my ideals of artist/educators and have my eternal respect. A shout out, too, to the fabulous WordCrew writers, past, present, and future—you're amazing to me. Keep it fresh, y'all!

My family has consistently believed in me and allowed me to follow my circuitous path through the years without raising too many eyebrows. To my mother Alice, my father Bernie, and my sisters Marci and Leslie— thank you for always being there when I come back home.

Ultimately, and most directly, it is the writers whose voices and experiences populate these pages who are responsible for this book. Ethnographic ethics require me to use pseudonyms, but you know who you are. To Crazy, Dave, José, Jig, Marta, Mekanismn, Patricia, TeTe, and Robbie—and to Leo, whose story I told in an early article—my eternal thanks. Your generosity in sharing your stories and your writing is . . . well, I just don't know what to say about it. Really—just thank you, thank you, thank you, and I hope I have come close to representing your experiences here in ways that seem fair and respectful.

——

A number of awards and grants have provided time and financial support during the drafting and revision of this book: at Louisiana State University, the LSU Council on Research Summer Stipend and a Faculty Research Grant, and at the University of Illinois at Chicago, the Robert Corley Memorial Scholarship, Rue Bucher Memorial Scholarship, English Graduate Student Research Bonus in Memory of Bernard R. Kogan, and Anne Hopewell Selby Award for distinction in graduate studies in English.

Several chapters in this book were published in earlier or partial form between 2005 and 2007. Chapter Five appeared under the same title in the journal *Written Communication* 24(1), pp. 28–48. Parts of Chapter Six appeared as "A love for the thing: The pleasures of rap as a literate discourse" in the *Journal of Adolescent and Adult Literacy* 50(4), pp. 270–281, and as "Free style: The role of play in rap composition" in the eBook *Creative engagements: Thinking with children 31*, pp. 103–106. Parts of Chapter Seven were published as "I shine with the rhythm: Rap writing, literate identity, and academic achievement" in the *International Journal of Learning 12*(3), pp. 143–147. Finally, some of the data from this research appeared in *very* early form as "The writing on the wall: Attending to self-motivated student literacies" in *English Education 35*(1), pp. 21– 45.

A number of popular song lyrics are quoted throughout this book. In several cases, I have stayed within Fair Use guidelines. For the lyrics that I quote at length, I have secured permission from the relevant music publishers, as follows:

Fear Not of Man
Words and Music by Dante Smith
©1999 EMI BLACKWOOD MUSIC INC., EMPIRE INTERNA-
TIONAL and MEDINA SOUND MUSIC
All Rights Controlled and Administered by EMI BLACKWOOD
MUSIC INC.
All Rights Reserved International Copyright Secured Used by Permission

Juicy
Words and Music by Sean Combs, Christopher Wallace, Jean Claude
Olivier, and James Mtume
©1994 EMI APRIL MUSIC INC., JUSTIN COMBS PUBLISHING
COMPANY INC., BIG POPPA MUSIC, JUMPING BEAN SONGS
LLC and MTUME MUSIC
All Rights for JUSTIN COMBS PUBLISHING COMPANY INC. and
BIG POPPA MUSIC Controlled and Administered by EMI APRIL
MUSIC INC.
All Rights Reserved International Copyright Secured Used by Permission
- contains elements of "Juicy Fruit"

Love
Words and Music by Dante Smith and Charles Njapa
©1999 EMI BLACKWOOD MUSIC INC., EMPIRE INTERNA-
TIONAL, MEDINA SOUNDS MUSIC and JANITORIAL DUTIES
All Rights for EMPIRE INTERNATIONAL and MEDINA SOUNDS
MUSIC Controlled and Administered by EMI BLACKWOOD MUSIC
INC.
All Rights Reserved International Copyright Secured Used by Permission

My Name Is
Words and Music by Labi Siffre
©1999 M.A.M. (MUSIC PUBLISHING) CORP.

Introduction

I always thought the stories I had in my head
were definitely better than those I've read. (Robbie)

Who wrote these rules?
Who formed these schools?
Teaching us Lincoln freed the slaves,
That Columbus discovered America . . .
(José)

I was master of the darkest art/since my birth
no time to focus on the afterlife/I'm bringing hell to earth
not because I'm a menace/but a talented individual
young, black, and gifted . . .
(Jig)

— —

I was a teenage writer.

I was also (a long time ago now) an unmotivated student attending a massive public high school of about 5,000 students, doing well in English but not much else, cutting more and more days as sophomore year turned to junior turned to senior, more interested in friends, music, and my own personal and family problems than in school assignments and grades.

I share this history because it has a lot to do with why this book exists. Given my background, it seems perfectly reasonable to me that someone can appear to be disengaged with school and with formal concepts of learning, yet be passionately involved in creative intellectual work. Despite the many differences between me and the nine writers in this study[1]—differences of cultural capital (if not socioeconomic status), race, (in some cases) gender, and geography—in significant ways, I *was* that teenager, less alienated than some of The Writers, certainly, but

1

more alienated than others. I get that what they present of themselves in the classroom—if they make it to the classroom at all—doesn't scratch the surface of who they are.

In this case, "who they are" are nine teenagers and young adults from Chicago: Jig, Mekanismn, Crazy, TeTe, Patricia, Marta, José, Robbie, and Dave.[2] There are connections and interconnections among some of them: Jig, Crazy, and TeTe are siblings; these three plus Mekanismn are part of a rap crew called The Maniacs; Patricia, Marta, José, Robbie, and Dave are all poets; and Mekanismn, Crazy, Patricia, Marta, José, and Robbie all attended an alternative high school on the south side of Chicago where each of them was, at one time or another, my student. The connection all nine share is that they fit into categories of youth too often represented— by the media, politicians, even the school systems that are supposed to serve them—as deficient in the kinds of characteristics and skills that both reflect and are supposed to lead to middle-class status. That is to say, each of The Writers is either African-American or Latino, all come from low-income families, and most of them have some difficulty writing formal academic essays and/or using standardized English in speech and in writing. To judge them as unskilled in reading and writing based solely on these measures, however, is to mistake form for content, the mastery of one grammatical system for an overall proficiency with communication, and a lack of interest in certain forms of literacy for a lack of interest in literacy generally. That such youth are immersed in various literate worlds exposes the narrowness of the definition of literacy within which our schools function, and requires an interrogation of the reasons that it is exactly the languages, the forms, and the styles of socially marginalized kids like these that don't count.

Each of The Writers composes in at least one of two general categories: poetry/narrative (I combine these under the general umbrella of "traditional" imaginative writing) and rap/hip-hop. Through interviews and observations, it has become clear that The Writers are motivated not by some romantic muse or inner voice of inspiration, but by the people, contexts, and situations that surround them. Some are influenced by the similar or complementary interests of family members. Some write in a kind of dialogue with published writing and/or recorded music. Some write as a way of verbalizing resistance to personal and societal issues. And many write with, for, and to their peers, bouncing rhymes off each other, sharing their poetry, and encouraging one another to keep writing.

In her article, "'To be part of the story': The literacy practices of gangsta adolescents," Elizabeth Moje (2000) defines what she calls the "alternative" or "unsanctioned" literacy practices of a group of young gang members with whom she works. Moje's important study is an early attempt to describe such literacy practices among this general demographic. Now, though, I hope to challenge the commonsense notion that academic literacies are the universal norm against which other practices are considered alternative. Instead, I argue that for adolescents, it is often the kinds of writing traditionally associated with formal schooling—what others have referred to as "academic" or "essayist" literacy—that are for many youths "alternative" and "unsanctioned." This is not always true—when students find themselves, in the classroom, able to draw on the rhetorical skills that they have developed through participation in discourses they value, the sense of alterity can dissipate. It seems obvious: young people can and do engage with writing, and often do it well, when they have a reason and when they can incorporate the skills they have developed through prior writing experiences. The fact that students' writing so often seems alternative and is, indeed, not sanctioned in their academic lives suggests not that *they* are doing something unusual, but that the schools are. Educators, policy makers, parents, and other adults who have young people's best interests at heart have a responsibility to educate themselves, to focus not only on what kids need to be taught, but on what makes them want to learn.

— —

La Juventud is a school for students aged 16 to 21 who have left high school for some period of time and have either decided or have been required to return. Because the public schools do not have to re-enroll a student once he/she turns 16, alternative schools like *La Juventud* are the only option for youth who want to earn a high school diploma rather than a G.E.D. Many of the students at this school have children; some have been or are currently involved in gang activities; some have been involved with the juvenile justice system. Many have a history of truancy, which in some cases doesn't end with their enrollment at *La Juventud*.

While *La Juventud* is not the central research site for this study, it is the place where I first encountered most of The Writers, first read their work, and carried out a number of interviews and observations. My access to this site comes from having been a full-time English teacher at the school for two years. During that period, I published several student literary magazines and newspapers that included work by Crazy and Mekanismn; Patricia was also a student in my classes at this time. I left that job to pursue a PhD, but throughout the course of my research, I continued to participate at the school as a librarian, a literacy resource, and a volunteer instructor. It was in writing workshops during this part-time involvement at *La Juventud* that I began to work with Robbie, Marta, and José's girlfriend Flor.

Moving beyond *La Juventud* for my research, I investigated the various contexts within which The Writers' literacy activities occurred, and that gave those activities their meaning. I followed participants into the community, to their homes, neighborhoods, community centers, and open mike events—to the places, in short, where their writing emerged.

In order to make sense of the meanings and contexts surrounding The Writers' work, I have relied principally upon the work done in New Literacy Studies (Barton, Hamilton & Ivanic, 2000; de Castell, Luke & Egan, 1986; Knobel, 1999; Gee, 1996; Street, 1995). Writers in this field argue that reading, writing, and verbal communication are all deeply contextualized activities that, as such, can only be understood by exploring the people, places, and powers that surround and infuse them. The field also emphasizes the multiple nature of literacy (hence the pluralizing of the term), challenging the traditional wisdom that one is either literate (meaning that one can read and write in the dominant linguistic codes) or illiterate. Particularly influential in this regard is Shirley Brice Heath's seminal 1983 ethnography *Ways With Words*—readers may notice this phrase used in various places throughout this book. I do this both because Heath's title is particularly apt in referring to literacy practices and because I want to pay respect to a work that has been foundational to literacy studies as a whole and to my own understanding of what literacy research grounded in specific social contexts requires.

Also central to this study is James Gee's (1996) concept of "Discourses," which refers to the social contexts of literacy acts—he uses the capital "D" to differentiate this concept from the linguistic definition of discourse as an extended speech event. I argue that for the writers in this study, literacy acts drive and are driven by their involvement in various dynamic Discourses. Gee's Discourse is both a context and a way of behaving within that context, "a sort of identity kit which comes complete with the appropriate costume and instructions on how to act, talk, and often write, so as to take on a particular social role that others will recognize . . ." (127–128). Of course, the metaphor of a "kit" suggests a more clear-cut set of discursive norms than actually exists. Nonetheless, the notion of Discourse is helpful in discussing the impact of race and ethnicity on individuals' experiences and opportunities in the U.S. It helps us to understand race and ethnicity as something other than static collections of characteristics that every person from a given group carries around with them in the same ways. There are not "race" and "ethnicity"; there are, instead, *Discourses* of race and ethnicity, some of which serve to essentialize and reify these concepts. There are all sorts of other Discourses as well; one of the best articulations of this concept that I have found comes from rapper Mos Def (1999a), who defines the Discourse of hip-hop this way:

> People be asking me all the time,
> "Yo Mos, what's getting ready to happen with Hip-Hop?
> Where do you think Hip-Hop is going?"
> I tell 'em, "You know what's gonna happen with Hip-Hop?
> Whatever's happening with us."
> If we smoked out, Hip-Hop is gonna be smoked out
> If we doing alright, Hip-Hop is gonna be doing alright
> People talk about Hip-Hop like it's some giant living in the
> hillside coming down to visit the townspeople—
> We *are* Hip-Hop.

Substitute whatever Discourse you choose for Mos Def's *hip-hop* and the argument still works. Discourses are ideologically fraught and politically contested, and some of them—like commercial rap music—generate serious profits, but they are also populated by individuals with histories and experiences that affect the Discourse as much as the Discourse influences the individual. It is for exactly this reason that Discourses—whether hip-hop, or the stock market, or public education—regularly feature heated debates over how, where, and by whom they should be represented.[3]

Another key theoretical concept undergirding this study is that of social reproduction. According to this idea, "ideological state apparatuses" (Althusser, 1977) such as the courts, churches, and schools work to reproduce class structures and social positioning. This implies that people are passive recipients and enactors of reproductive ideologies. However, a number of researchers (Cushman, 1998; de Certeau, 1984; Ogbu, 1991; Scott, 1990; Spivak, 1999; Williams, 2002) have uncovered past and present enactments of agency on the part of dominated and marginalized peoples. In terms of literacy, because one's verbal performances are tied up with one's relationships and sense of self, one may resist participation in a (socially sanctioned) Discourse that conflicts with other (less socially valued) Discourses with which one identifies. A number of first- and second-hand accounts tell of the alienation that can result from moving between a home and a school that are grounded in highly contrastive language and literacy norms (Anzaldua, 1987; Delpit, 1995; Rodriguez, 1993; Rodriguez, 1982; Rose, 1990; Villanueva, 1993). Pierre Bourdieu (1990), writing about a school system's "social function of conservation and . . . ideological function of legitimation" (102), warns against ignoring these conflicts, and the resistant stances that may develop from them, if one wants to get to the root of problems within the educational system.

Such conflicts generate tension because the languages they are rooted in are always rooted in power. Mikhail Bakhtin (1981) celebrated what he termed the *heteroglossia* (the many and varied ways with words) of democratic societies; his writings critique the stifling of heteroglossia in the Soviet Union in which he lived. Although he was writing in response to a specific historical context, Bakhtin's mistrust of societies' tendency to naturalize the dominance of some Discourses over others is directly and powerfully relevant to current discussions of the ways that racially and economically marginalized people speak and write.

Because of its emphasis on language as an inherently social act, this study runs the risk of missing the trees for the forest, as it were. Individuals experience themselves as individuals, no matter how many books are written about the social construction of identity and culture. This is especially true in the United States, which is predicated on a belief in the primacy of the individual. On the other hand, when motivations are looked for within individual minds, social context often disappears. The field of social psychology wrestles with the intersections of individual and social experience. One figure who informs this study from the perspective of social psychology is Lev Vygotsky (1986). This Soviet educator-turned-psychologist viewed a science of the mind that distinguishes itself from the social as fundamentally flawed, based as it must be on an assumption that the individual can be understood apart from the society he/she inhabits.

Looking at the variety of data generated by my research, both during the active research process and during postresearch analysis, I was able to identify a number of central themes. My own experiences as a teacher, writer, and researcher suggested to me that there is no fundamental correspondence between an engagement with imaginative writing outside of school and academic success—whether measured in grades, test scores, or evident mastery of the grammatical/syntactical tools of standardized English. This situation calls for intensive scrutiny not only of schooling, but of the contexts in which such youth *do* engage productively with intellectual work. Yet there are "only a few studies of how marginalized adolescents . . . use literacy to make sense of their social and school lives" (Moje, 2000, 653). The present study demonstrates that such teenagers and young adults are often deeply engaged in writing, so the low performance of many such youth in school settings presents us with a conundrum. Why doesn't their intense interest in writing translate to school achievement? That they learn not only how to write, but how to think critically and analyze audiences from their crafting of poems and song lyrics is clear from the way they talk about their work in this book. The conclusion I and others (see Mahiri, 2004) come to is that the difference lays in the level of connection youth feel to the writing they choose to do—in other words, the extent to which these literate practices are woven into the cultural and social contexts of their lives.

Searching for answers in interview transcripts, field notes, and the writing itself, I found that general themes of *control, internal exploration, interpersonal interaction, challenge, respect,* and *enjoyment* came up repeatedly. These themes were often inseparable from one another—as in, for example, *challenges* that involve *competition with peers* in an *enjoyable atmosphere* with the *respect of valued others* as the reward. In an effort to create a text that allows for both organizational clarity and contextual complexity, I chose to break these themes into chapters that include discussions of that thematic interplay.

While this book is unapologetically an examination of particular situated literacy practices, I have tried to be mindful of recent critiques of literacy ethnographies. By definition, all New Literacy Studies work is firmly grounded in the local and particular, as Sheridan, Street, and Bloome remind us: "The challenge for researchers interested in literacy is to describe the social, cultural and intellectual events and practices within which written language is used" (2000, 5). Both Collins and Blot (2003) and Brandt (2001) acknowledge the value of situated studies, but express concern that a preoccupation with local practices often obscures larger socioeconomic factors driving particular orientations to literacy. Brandt, in particular, is concerned that a focus on how individuals and communities employ particular literacy practices to achieve specific goals ignores the reality that literacy practices are often not so much chosen as they are inherited, assumed, or imposed—and this is true not only for those practices that are overtly "oppressive," but to some extent for all practices. "Ethnographic descriptions," says Brandt,

> do not often speak directly enough and in a sustained way to the histories by which literacy practices arrive or do not arrive in local contexts, flourish or not in certain times and locales. Nor do they often invite a search for the interests beyond those of the local users that hold literacy practices in place, give them their meaning, or take them away. Nor do they often fully address the mixed motives, antipathies, and ambivalence with which so much literacy is learned and practiced. (2001, 8)

This book, therefore, moves back and forth between macro and micro, between the practices of the nine featured writers and the ideological, political, and economic conditions that frame their particular practices. This book is based on a belief that there continues to be value in documenting the richness of "unofficial" literacies, but that to do so without contextualizing these practices within larger social/economic/historical forces is ultimately of limited use.

Reflecting these complementary concerns, the first two chapters provide both micro- and macro-overviews of the book's major themes. First, readers are introduced to each of The Writers and read a piece of writing from each. The greatest pleasure for me in doing this work has been getting to know The Writers; the greatest challenge, to present them in these pages as multidimensional individuals with experiences and practices that are simultaneously representative of similarly positioned youth and deeply personal. I hope that these initial descriptions will give readers some sense of who The Writers are as individuals, and will enrich readers' understandings of the chapters that follow.

Moving out from the individual, we look next at the historical and contemporary interplay among language, literacy, and the people who enact them. Readers are introduced to or reminded of the Ebonics controversy of the 1990s, cross-generational and cross-racial attitudes toward rap music, and efforts to legislate the language of *latinidad*.[4]

Having established these larger frameworks, we then begin to explore the themes reflected in The Writers' work. I start with an examination of the role imaginative writing plays as a relatively safe site for identity development and identity play. I use the term "identifications" to highlight the ways that teenagers play off of people, images, and ideas with which they connect for a variety of reasons, and the term "communality" (which strikes me as a less fixed, more experiential term than "community") to express the feeling of connection and inclusion that writing in certain genres—such as rap—provides young people when they perceive themselves to be participants in a public and well-populated discourse. In addition, there is discussion of the ways that writing gives these youth confidence, respect, and certain kinds of cultural capital, while the very same writing—because of the dialect in which it is written and/or the subject matter it broaches—can simultaneously serve to reinforce stereotypes of urban youth and reinscribe their subordinate social positions.

While concepts such as identification and communality provide general frameworks for understanding The Writers' methods and choices, there are specific kinds of identity and social work being done by their composing practices that warrant particular attention. Engagements with varying formulations of gender and sexuality are apparent in much of The

Writers' work, so I look closely at the ways that The Writers at times reinforce, and at times confound, common conceptions of the connections between writing and gender. I pay special attention to the ways that The Writers work through and experiment with gender roles in their writing, and address such issues as the role of sexuality in popular rap lyrics and what the rappers in this study *do* with what they are hearing.

All of these rather serious questions lead next to a deeply important, but often overlooked, element of imaginative writing—the satisfaction, pride, or sheer fun that one experiences in doing it. Pleasure as a goal in and of itself has always been controversial, yet I argue that some form of pleasure is fundamental to meaningful intellectual and imaginative work.

Having contextualized The Writers' practices from these many and varied perspectives, we are now ready to move to questions of learning and of specific composing practices. My aim is to demonstrate that learning is a process (or, really, a myriad of interweaving processes) that cannot be fully understood or deeply supported without the kind of larger examinations that are the focus of most of the book. Having come to this juncture, we look at both how and what the writers learn about the composing process through their imaginative writing. I offer examples of both collaboration and apprenticeship as learning models that young writers engage in. I also demonstrate the various features of imaginative writing—literary techniques, writing process, attention to audience—that are evident in the work of The Writers and in the ways they talk about that work.

Finally, I address the question always on the tip of the classroom teacher's tongue: "What does this mean for me and my students?" I suggest ways that an understanding of youths' out-of-school writing practices can inform and enrich the ways that teachers discuss writing in school, and can shift their perceptions of students from individuals who know little or nothing about the "right" way to write to people who have deep funds of knowledge on which to draw as they negotiate various forms of composition. I also discuss powerful teen literacy work being done outside of formal school settings, and suggest ways that educators can shift their self-conceptions from classroom teacher to literacy educator, which involves movement beyond classroom walls and an active engagement with all of the complexities of literacy learning and its sociocultural implications.

Because The Writers are so central to this study and this book, because their voices infuse every page, and because so much time has passed since the moment I first began transcribing Mekanismn's scribbled rhymes on the *La Juventud* library computer at lunch and publishing Crazy's earliest poems in the school literary magazine, the book ends where it began, with The Writers themselves, this time looking at where they are in their lives and work at press time. As readers will see, much has changed, and some has not. I hope that the sheer variety of The Writers' stories will encourage readers to look at every young person they encounter with the assumption that they have a rich imaginative life, however active or dormant, and that our responsibility as adults is to encourage that life.

1

"I Am Me But Who Am I?"

INTRODUCING THE WRITERS

I've been thinking recently about what it means to be a writer, how it feels, why it happens. Partly, this is because of the research for this book. But I've also been doing more writing myself in the last few years than I have for a very long time. To be sure, it's been mostly academic writing, but I've been able to work within that genre without entirely giving up the cool part—the thinking about sound, about telling stories, about creating a text that feels something like part of a conversation. I was excited the first time an article I wrote was published in a respected journal—but I was also a bit deflated when I realized that the responses I was getting during the revision process would peter out after publication. Journals don't have letters-to-the-editor sections; they don't have huge circulations, and if someone assigns your piece as a class reading, odds are you'll never know.

In June of 2003, though, I finally got a chance. A friend teaching a graduate education seminar at Elmhurst College assigned my article to her class as one of several ethnographic literacy studies they were reading. She invited me to visit one Thursday evening. The students—all teachers themselves—had enough questions that there was never an awkward silence; they seemed interested in what I had to say; they referred to specific passages in the article that they particularly liked. It felt like I was finally getting a response to a question I had thrown out months before.

From January to May of the same year, I taught one of two sections of a methods course on the teaching of writing in the high schools. Around mid-term, as the capper to a unit on teaching and writing poetry, the classes combined for a poetry reading. We held the reading in the back room of a local bar, the same room where members of the university's creative writing program hold regular readings. As our students arrived, they stopped at the bar to order drinks and snacks, then filtered into the room to grab a seat at one of several round tables. There was a small stage up front with a chair and a microphone. One by one, we called each student up to read. Some were relaxed, some nervous—and some really, really didn't want to go. But everyone read, and everyone said they were glad afterward.

I was one of the last to read. I didn't feel nervous until I got in front of everyone; suddenly, I was self-conscious—what if they didn't like it? They would pretend they did, of course, but what if they didn't really? And how could I start? How could I open my mouth and commit to saying the words that I had crafted into this poem about war and fear and connection? It's like the moment when you stand at the edge of a diving board, staring down . . . it's not fear exactly, or if it is, it's a fear not of harm but of commitment. You are conscious that there is a choice, and that one choice will keep you up here, dry and safe, while the other will send you plunging through the air with no control over anything, until you slice into the water and pop up again through its surface. You know that if you do it, you'll be okay, but you also know that you're about to willingly, if temporarily, sacrifice control.

I read, of course. And I enjoyed it in a way it hadn't occurred to me that I would. I left the stage wanting to do it again and again. I wanted to run home, jump on the Internet and find the listings for local open mikes where I could keep saying things to people and watching and hearing and feeling them respond. What I was feeling, I realize now, is not very different from what The Writers had described to me over and over again—I enjoyed the individual writing of my poem, yes, but even more, I liked the performance, the response, and the thrill of jumping in.

— —

This book is about writers. Some write poems and show them to friends, some compose rap lyrics and trade freestyles (impromptu raps) back and forth. All of them *want* to write, *choose* to, and *continue* choosing to. It has been odd for me at times to be a researcher among them, to study creative writing in particular, without being one of the ones doing it. I have felt like a fraud, like an outsider, talking the talk without walking the walk, claiming to know something about writing without offering any evidence. None of the writers ever asked me for any—they're good people, polite, and it may not seem obvious that the adult with the tape recorder and a whole university backing her up should have to prove that she knows what she's talking about and can understand what they're saying.

Around 3 a.m. one morning, though, I had this Instant Messenger conversation with one of The Writers:

Crazy: Hey, Sue, why don't you create a name on the boards?
SW: On which boards? The Keys?
Crazy: Yep.
SW: Why?
Crazy: You like to write. Why don't you freestyle sometimes?
SW: Oooooohhhh.
SW: Yikes. I've never even tried freestyling.
SW: It's a little intimidating.
Crazy: Nah, nah, it's not intimidating. Besides you've done it before.
SW: When?
Crazy: Whenever you write the first thoughts comes from the top [of your head].
Crazy: Think about it.
SW: I will. I see what you mean . . .
SW: I guess what I've never tried is writing to a hip-hop beat . . . 'cause that's what everyone on the boards seems to do.
Crazy: Nah, that's just us most of the time. SP, Ambishn, and Kim go a capella.
Crazy: Or you can flow to some of the music that you got. You know, bring a new flava in it.
SW: And I guess I could always just not send something if it didn't seem to work . . .
SW: It would actually be cool to try. I think I just might.
Crazy: Yeah. Yeah, go for it, go for it, you can do it, *sí se puede*!
SW: Okay, Cesar Chavez.
Crazy: LOL.

Telling a friend at work about this today, I said, "The student has become the master." But I was never the master—they've been the ones doing all the writing, not me—and if any of the writers in this study have been my students, it's only ever been partial. I won't deny that there are things I know, skills I have, that they don't. I have many years more experience reading and critiquing a variety of writing, for example; after all this time, it's also fair to say that I am familiar with the norms of a broader range of Discourses. And I'm afraid that I am, as one of my college students announced not too long ago, something of a "grammar wonk." But it's clear that they have much to teach me as well.

So now I'm a novice on the boards, writing a rhyme and then checking back far too often to see if anyone's said anything about it. And that anticipation and rush and desire to write more, that feeling of now being able to talk on the boards because I'm writing too, makes me realize that to have written this book without becoming a writer again myself would have resulted in something perhaps interesting, but also perhaps empty, lacking a real understanding of what it feels like to write to and with others. That is, after all, the experience at the heart of this study.

My first post on the Alicia Keys website message boards
04:41am Jul 9, 2003 EST

```
It's rough trying to write a page on a new stage
I'm a poet on paper but I'm in a new phase.
Not a rhymer by nature but I'll give it a go
'Cause the more that you try, the more that you know.
In the company of strangers but you all don't seem strange,
Except that your rhymes cover such a broad range-it's the
language that matters, and the things that we say
the sound and the fury, not black/white but gray.
Gray matters, gray matter is where it all starts,
it comes from the head, it comes from the heart.
Now it's late, my brain's tired, it's time for some rest. I
can sleep now I've finished, I've passed my own test.
```

CRAZY

> "Remember me, I'm B—, a.k.a. Lyrical, a.k.a. Crazy the Lyrical
> Sage, also known as Crazy Boy."

I've known Crazy for about four years. When I taught at *La Juventud* (*LJ*), he was the youngest student there. Officially, the school was not supposed to admit anyone under the age of 16—the legal age at which one could leave school. Crazy was 15 when he entered; I never knew how this happened, but as a result of his youth and his cheerful innocence, he became a favorite of the teachers. We would take turns driving him home after school, since he had been threatened several times when he walked. The principal at the time worried that we might be coddling him when we should be encouraging him to develop strategies for confronting the dangers from which we could not, after all, always protect him.

Crazy left every term-end awards assembly laden with certificates, and he consistently earned top grades. He was and is unfailingly polite;

the only context in which I have heard him say negative things about anyone is when he is doing battle through his rap lyrics. I found out, though, that this was not always the case, as his younger sister TeTe revealed during an interview at which she, Crazy, and their older brother Jig were present:

Jig: It depends on where Crazy's at. He can be a [inaudible].
TeTe: He used to be—
Crazy: Hey, hey, hey, most of the time—
TeTe: He's different than he used to be.
Crazy: But *very* seldom.
TeTe: When he was this small, the boy, you could say hi to him the wrong way, he'd be like, "What'd-you-say-hi-to-me-for?"
Crazy: [inaudible]
TeTe: Oh you calling me a dog now?
Crazy: I was a short, mad, skinny, little person.
TeTe: He was a nerd. But no one would mess with him. He was a strong nerd. Where the picture at? Pop bottle glasses and all, crusty lips . . .
Everyone laughs.

Crazy started writing during his second year at *LJ*: "I was given the challenge to write a poem one time, and I liked the challenge. Next thing I knew, I was writing, and kept writing . . ." As he talks, I realize that the poem he's referring to as his first is, in fact, the poem he contributed to the first official literary magazine I published there as a full-time teacher. It was a template-poem; starting in the first line with the phrase "I Am," each line began with a set introductory phrase with the writer filling in the rest:

I am a native but what type,
I am Black but from who or of what form,
I am white but of which race,
I am me but who am I?

I am a puddle of mud in the form of a body,
I am a pile of bones created from fossils,
I am water from the earth which keeps me moist,
I am a spirit from the soul of the earth,
I am me but what does it mean?

I am white which brings light upon me,
I am a form of dignity and inspiration,
I am a form which brings good quality and awareness to others,
I am a form of hope of one who cares,
I am me or who am I?
I am all cultures, of all races
I am me or who am I,
I am nature that is me and that is who I am.

His version caught my eye when I first saw it posted with others on the English classroom wall. After the book came out, I learned from Gina—

SOUL SEARCHER

The seekers
Of the darkness
Labeled my unpaved
Carcass
Who am I?
Just another product
Or a glare
Of a starter
Redeparted from the core
That betrothed my heart
Pounding agony
Wretched scars
And punishing flaws
Surrounded in the stall
Damn, where's or is this my calling
Grouping thoughts
But nonsense
Is what I sought
Warmth and cold coughs
Sickening the cove
Stone walls
With miniature circle holes
A frozen pose
That can't be unthawed
Or can it . . .
Maybe it's just an unjust cause
But then why do silence pause

Why do noise disrupt
Why do light blind
And why do nights blacken
The metaphoric phrases
Betray and escalate
Each timing of a change
While the time at hand
By passes and never
Retracts its selfish hand
Nor reaches back to gather
Its unseen chance
But stays banned
And leaves the sightings
To the walking hanker
And leads lost puzzles to a pale moon
So they can dance
An enhanced
Laboratory
Exposes some truths
Of history
But never completely
Exerts itself
In anguished deficiency
Animosity holographs
Like a mirage
To keep cold water
In the mouth of the ones that's hot

the other English teacher and the one with whom Crazy had the closest relationship—that Crazy was upset because the last line of his poem was incorrect in the book. I felt terrible, and apologized to him at the first opportunity. He was gracious, of course, and said it was no big deal.

I no longer feel quite so bad about having misquoted that poem, because Crazy has gone on to write so many more poems and raps, and has found his own ways of making them public. While Crazy does a lot of creative work (graphic design, playing the keyboard), he says that he has found certain specific satisfactions in writing: "You can take certain things that [happen in] life and alter them into a different certain way. It's like a puzzle, you gotta piece everything together, and if you don't get it, you won't understand it, and if you don't look deep enough inside it, you won't get the true meaning."

DAVE

"I guess I'll be finished when I'm dead."

E-mail from me to Eva 7–11–03:

I have to go tomorrow at 11 to interview a 20-year-old named Dave about his writing. He made the terrible mistake of calling up the Writing Center[2] to see if he could bring his poetry in to have someone look at it. One of my students was working with him, and she came over to Naomi and me in the middle of the hour to ask if we had suggestions for where this guy could get poems published. She brought him over, and as we started talking to him, the tentacles slithered out of my head and poked around, sensing research material nearby. I asked him more and more questions: "What are you doing now? Do you go to school? Do other people in your family write? Can I see some of your poems?" Finally, I had to 'fess up to what I was doing; Naomi and Heather had seen it coming from a mile away. So I explained my project, apologized several times for taking him over and turning him into a text, popped his diskette into the computer (a Writing Center no-no), clicked on the categories he indicated and the poem titles he pointed out, and read. He said he has something like 137 poems—he counted. And he has them all on his disk organized by categories (Love, Fake Friends, and so on). So I asked if I could

interview him; he said sure, all he's doing currently is
writing, babysitting, and playing basketball. His
brother has triplets (!!!!!), so he helps to take care
of them, trading off with his mom and, I guess, said
brother. He was going to one of the City Colleges, but
he didn't like it. And he plays basketball with guys
from the neighborhood in the evening; he likes it that
sometimes, the ones who aren't playing sit on the bench
and talk about all sorts of things.

And his parents are from Peru. He's only been there
once, but he said it was good for him to see what's considered a third world country; he said that a lot of the
guys in his neighborhood don't know that there's anything
beyond the neighborhood, which is why they might just as
well get involved in gangs or whatever—which makes
sense, if they think that it's no different anywhere
else. His sister goes to the university, studies Latin
American history and politics. He said he doesn't get
along with her very well. Apparently, she's very involved
in Latino identity/political stuff, which grates on him,
even though he seems to also have fairly lefty views. We
talked about how identifying oneself primarily by race or
ethnicity can be a trap, and can powerfully exclude
others or cause narrowing, rigid definitions of what it
means to be of a given race/ethnicity. Those may be more
my words than his, but he had these ideas too. And he
said that the problem is that his sister's worldview
doesn't allow for contradictions. I thought that was very
smart, since I'm starting to see contradiction as basically at the heart of every damn thing.

As you may have noticed, this has ceased to be an
email and has become instead a convenient, non-work-
feeling way of starting to write up field notes, which
I've been meaning to do since Thursday. So sorry, and
thanks.

7/12/03—Post interview email to Eva:
I interviewed the guy that I told you about yesterday.
It is incredible how open someone will be about his life
to me when we met only three days ago. He told me about

his schooling, his difficult relationships with his
family, his depression, his 5 days in jail, watching a
friend get shot as he was crossing the street to meet
him, writing a letter to the principal of his Catholic
high school complaining that there was no "world" in the
world history class and then getting enraged and knock-
ing stuff off the assistant principal's desk when the
man smirked as he read the letter. The poor guy had been
in the emergency room all night with a bacterial infec-
tion; he had a 105 fever and had been sick for two days
before, so he was on maybe a couple hours sleep when I
arrived. But we talked for a good two hours.

Anyway, he's going to come to the Writing Center on
Wednesday so we can look at his poems together—he's
never really gotten constructive criticism on his writing, so I'll have to go slow, but I'm glad there's something I can do to return the favor.

— —

Dave's sense of himself as a writer is reflected in the way he represents himself when I ask him how he gets ideas for writing:

I usually get ideas from anywhere. I'll be taking a shower, and an idea will come to me, and I'll have to run out and write it down before I forget. And then finish it off, driving—it's probably worse than talking on a cell phone, 'cause I'm trying to write; I don't want to lose the idea. But also my mom and dad, friends, will see me with all this writing on my arm. I'll forget to wash it off, so I'll have it all over my arm. People will say, "Oh, is that gang?" and I'll say, "No gang writes on their arm. They're not that educated."

Dave *is* that educated, reading the dictionary and constantly searching the Internet for cool articles. I got this e-mail from him a few months after he moved to Miami to live with his cousins:

I went to the library yesterday and took out a library
card. I took out five books right away:
1 is the *Autobiography of Malcom X* by Alex Haley, 2 was
a book on Frederick Douglass (really thick), 3 was a

book entitled *Violence* (violence in American society), 4
is a biography on Gandhi (also thick), and 5 is a book
called *Armed and Dangerous*, it's memoirs of a Chicago
cop working the southwest side (I wonder if the title
describes the gangbangers, the streets, or the cops). I
also put a book on hold called *The Art of War*. Have you
read any of these wonderfully delightful brightly . . .
books? Too many adjectives that make no damn sense.
Well, I'll talk to you later. Stay up. I'm out.

"CRAZY HORSE"

Mestizo

    Language

       Blood

         Pizarro

          Alamo

           Immigration

            Prison

              History

               Che

                 Raped

Mulatto   Prison   Hip-hop   Spic

  Dialect   Reagan   Welfare   History   Raped   Nigger   You

    Slavery   Malcolm   Cracker

                 Raped

              Vanity

            History

          Bail

        Liberty

      Crown

     Auschwitz

   Oppressor

  Tongue

Albino

JIG

"I'm so far ahead of my time . . ."

I've always been into music to begin with, but I started writing poetry in second grade. Ever since then I've been getting better and better, and when I got into high school, I started winning contests, like whenever I would enter a contest with my poetry I would always win, so people would always tell me I need to get my poetry published and have a book or something like that. And then my friends, they was already rapping, and they told me that since I had been writing poetry for so long, that it's basically rap. Just have to put it to a flow, or put it to a beat. And so I did it, like, a couple times, then we made a couple songs, and then they let people hear 'em; they was like, "You good, you ought to keep on going."

Jig is Crazy's older brother, and the acknowledged leader of their musical/entrepreneurial group, The Maniacs. His younger sister TeTe likens Jig's role in the group to that of a father. He takes care of the business—when I tell him, on Instant Messenger, that I'll need them to sign photo releases, he says that he'll need to look the document over: "You know I don't sign anything without reading it." When I drop the photo CD and the release off a few weeks later, I jokingly say, "Here you go. Have your lawyer look it over, and let me know if you want anything changed." To which he responds, "I *am* the lawyer."

I first met Jig one afternoon in the summer of 2002, when he, Crazy, TeTe, Mekanismn, and two other friends were hanging out in one of the small basement studios of the community youth radio station where most of them were taking classes. What struck me about Jig at that first meeting was his familiarity and confidence—he immediately started talking to me, asking questions, not worrying about whether I would find any of them awkward or invasive. As I've gotten to know him, I've come to understand that this is part of his overall sense of himself—some of it is bravado, certainly, but there is also a core of sureness in him about his intelligence, his talent, and his potential. When I ask him, for instance, what he's majoring in at school, he responds: "Technological engineering, computer programming, business management, and creative writing. I have two majors and two minors. I'm gonna be in school forever." Now, I had three majors in college, but they were consecutive, not simultaneous.

The mix of confidence and competition that informs much of what Jig does is apparent when I ask him how he got started writing in second grade . . .

As far as schoolwork, I've always thought a lot. . . . My writing, it wasn't really that good back then ((laughs)), it was like putting stuff together, like making things. I wanted to be like the top person, so I always had to think about things . . .

. . . and when I suggest that with all the subjects he's studying in college, he must be doing schoolwork constantly:

Honestly, I don't have to study a lot. Because I catch on so easy, and I memorize so easy, and then whenever we got papers due, I always do 'em maybe thirty, twenty minutes before class. And people usually get upset about it, 'cause I'll still get an A on the paper ((laughs)). So they used to get mad. They'd say, "I been doing this paper for three weeks, and I just got a C+."

Here, TeTe chimes in with mock resentment: "And I somehow get a C."
This is not to say that Jig believes everything he does is perfect. During another Instant Messenger conversation (Jig and I shared a tendency to be up late into the night, so our IM exchanges became fairly common), he admits that there are always some poems and some lyrics that he doesn't like. But he handles this in typical fashion:

```
Jig says:
     i usually just put it with the rest of the stuff,
     it's all my thoughts at the spur of moment, so i'm
     still happy with it, i might use some of the con-
     cepts or parts in later stuff that i write
sueweinst says:
     Yeah, makes sense. Kind of like a writer's notebook.
Jig says:
     yeah, and besides like jay-z said
     "I'm so far ahead of my time
     These rhymes is weak
     Till four years later,
     they on time release"
sueweinst says:
     Man, you are full of . . .
sueweinst says:
     confidence.
Jig says:
     lol
Jig says:
```

"that's when they realize that every line need an
autopsy, the more flows mean the more bodies, and if
you don't listen further then you're missing a
murder, don't you know my worst flow, is better than
your best, my lyrical bullets make you wear a vest."

(from the Alicia Keys website message boards)
Jig (of The Maniacs)—09:01am Jul 8, 2003 EST

ayo, try to feel where i'm coming from with this one
ayo
I wanna thank god for America, but they treatin' me wrong
it's a shame, can't even find peace in this land that's home
how am I supposed to prosper, when the system against me
when the politicians smile in my face, but they really resent me
when the news push stereotypes
that we all gangstas and drugged up hypes
I know you feel these words, if you know what it's like
whether you black, brown, yellow, confused, or white
we all got despairities, that need to come from the dark to the
light
my fam gone live easy, even if i gotsta to chill in hell
I can take the torture and pain, as long as my kids live well
I got the mind of a scholar, but the heart of a fool
between my eyes, in my skull, lies the most deadliest tool
not just a brain, but a mind and a soul
that refuse to lose in America, the land of the barren and cold
let me except the sins of the father, I'm sacrificial to you
I know you speak through me, but I put my faith unto you
some people ain't gone be satisfied, till I'm stiff and I'm dead
I got big shoes to fill, can't let it get to my head
this battle for equality, is far from dead
whatever happened to democracy, they chose Bush instead
the richer getting richer, the economy dead
well at least for the poor, but we gone find solitude when our
last tears are shed
'cause on the cross next to Jesus was a crook and a thief
on the cross to his left, the man said, "Jesus forgive Me"
and into heaven he went, for repentin' his wrong deeds
who is last shall become first, that's what the psalms read
So thank you America, for all of your wrong deeds.

JOSÉ

"If I don't write, I'm gonna have all these burdens inside of me."

The first time I became aware of José was when he was accused of stealing money from a student's backpack. He wasn't enrolled at *La Juventud*, but as a resident in the agency's group home, he wandered around freely, hanging out in the reception area with students during lunch, walking through the administrative hallway looking for the group home "mom."

The truth is, José's hard to miss. He's a beefy kid, but what's hard to ignore is his head. It seems a little too big, oddly flat and round. And in the middle of it is the nose—big, misshapen, pushed in on one side. I remember the last time he broke it—he had become an *LJ* student at this point; he showed up for class with white gauze taped across the nose, with scratches and bruises on his cheeks and chin and under his eyes. He explained that he had been riding his bike around the park when he took a spill and landed smack on his face.

José became part of this project after his girlfriend, Flor, showed me his poems. Flor was in my creative writing class. She didn't show up a lot, but there was a couple-week stretch when she was attending pretty regularly. And José, who's only taking one class this term, would come to my class to do a little writing and talk to her. One class period, as I was checking in with her to see if she needed help with the story she was writing, she opened her binder and pulled out several pieces of paper with poems typed them. I read through them, surprised by their skill and thoughtfulness. And I remembered the first time José had given me a poem. He was in one of my English classes, and was responding to a call I had put out in the morning's announcements for writing to include in the literary magazine. I had taken the paper he handed me and read it in front of him. I don't remember the specific words of praise I used, but I know that even as I was saying them, in my head I was thinking, "He didn't write this. He couldn't write this. He stole this like he stole that student's money. I can't say that to him. But I can't put this in the magazine either."

I am now, very belatedly, learning how wrong I was, that in fact there's nothing about that flat face, that dented nose, that somewhat lumbering body, that precludes the existence of a writer inside. And although I know that I asked José if I could interview him for my research because of the proliferation and quality of his writing, maybe it was also a little bit because I had doubted him before. I'm not particularly proud to admit to these prejudices on my part, but I don't think it's terribly uncommon for adults to make assumptions about the youth they encounter based on things like appearance, the youth's history, the things we've heard.

So José and I sit in the student lounge, at one end of a long table. The big room is empty for the moment, although I worry that random students will wander in to get something from a locker while we're talking. But José seems pretty comfortable; I find with him what I've found with other student writers I've talked to recently—they've already thought about their writing, what they get from it, when it's mattered and how and why. And what I learn from José is that writing has been, since about age 11, one of the things that's gotten him through the kind of childhood that . . . well, that I don't know what to say about. Just leave a big blank here for things that I don't want to guess at and don't know for sure.

José tells me that he started writing when he was at the juvenile detention center. A speaker visited one day, a guy from "the 'hood" who was going to tell stories from a book he had written about his life, thus motivating the young offenders to change their ways. "Inspired Straight," you might say. Anyway, it pissed José off that this guy thought he was some kind of example that they should follow. So he thought to himself, "If that guy can write a book, I can write something better." And he started writing, pages and pages. And he found that it helped, pouring out all the stuff about his father, his family, abuse . . . Much later, he would find himself on a bus headed to County after an arrest, and he would find that he began to go crazy with no paper and pen, and he would wonder what would have happened to him if he had never had any.

Which is a good question, since even with writing to get him through some hard times, he also found himself in the hospital once. At this point, Flor has joined us in the lounge; she sits on a cushioned chair by the wall, watching and listening as we talk. I retroactively imagine a look passing between them when I ask José why he was in the hospital. He pauses, and I suddenly realize that I shouldn't have asked that at all. But then he says, "It was when I tried to kill myself."

Which brings me back to his nose. Because it had already looked pretty bad before he took that spill on the bike, and when he told me about that fall, his biggest frustration was that of all the places he could have injured, it had to be the one place that had already been hurt several times. And now I can't help but wonder how all of these stories are related. I think about the personal history he carries on his face, and about how he lost all of the poems and stories and journals he had written during his stints in the detention center and at the group home on the day he moved out, when someone stole his suitcase as it sat unattended on the stairs. I thought this was bad, but he said he didn't care. He said they were all about his family, and he could never be upset about losing things connected to them. And I realize that there are some stories he can choose to tell, some passions he can decide whether or not to communicate in his poems. And then there's the history he can't control, the one that his body carries whether he likes it or not.

"Rebel Against Morals"

Who wrote these rules?
Who formed these schools?
Teaching us Lincoln freed the slaves,
that Columbus discovered America.
To learn about some great military leader,
who killed off my ancestors,
His face resides on the twenty dollar bill.
Why learn all about this bullsh*t?
Will it put money in my pocket?
A roof above my head?
Hell no
F*cking hypocrites pumping the enemy into my brain.
All of them are scared.
Trying to put me to sleep,
None of them will ever phase me,
Just create me
To grow stronger
To rebel longer
And faster.

MARTA

"Sometimes when I feel sad or lonely I like to express myself through poems."

Marta was in the same creative writing class as Robbie (whom you'll meet soon) during the winter of 2002–2003. I interviewed her at school, sitting in a stairwell—the only empty space we could find. My tape of the interview is filled with our conversation, then the sound of a door opening, a disembodied voice apologizing, and stairs creaking as Marta and I shift to make room for the feet that press onto wooden steps, causing them to crunch like the back of an old man slowly standing.

To me, Marta's strongest physical attribute is her deep dimples; every time she smiles or laughs, I am taken aback by how sweet and young they make her look. But then, I have also seen Marta lose her temper, spending a class period yelling at Robbie and accusing him of staring at her, which of course made him stare at her more. And then, sometimes, she can tell the most painful stories all the way through in incredible detail as though she is reading from images burned into her mind. As we sat in a stairwell, she told me the story of the friend she lost when she was nine years old. She stared straight ahead, speaking as though in a trance, reciting the details almost as though they were lines from a story she's already written. She tells me this story to explain how she started to write: "When I was nine, turning ten, my best friend killed himself. His mom wanted me to make a speech about him. I didn't know what to write, so I made up a poem."

Her writing seems to have continued in this vein, as a way to work through feelings and experiences. She says, "Some of my poems are nice, too. I sometimes express my childhood through it too. I only live with my mom; I don't live with my dad. My dad left us when I was about five, and my mom became a father and mother to me. She had to raise four girls on her own. And [as] I grew up, my mom taught me not to hate my father. And not to judge him for what he did to us . . .

"I grew up being strong. I been through a lot, but I'm still strong and I keep my head up high. I'm not gonna let other people put me down. Since I was six, sometimes I get really stressed out; I get really sad. And sometimes I feel like giving up. Sometimes I even feel like crying like a little girl. But I stay strong, and I keep my head up high, and don't let it get to me."

False Homies

Cruising around town with my so called homies,
We see a rival,
BANG BANG—he's dead.
My homies tricked me,
But I was not the trigger,
Now I'm behind some bars for 10 years.
I'm only 16 years old wasting away for someone else's crime.
Dedicated to all my forgotten homies in jail

[Marta wrote this for two male friends who served time in jail for a robbery: "Nobody bothered to visit them," she says. She sent each of them a copy of the poem.]

MEKANISMN

"That's what I do every day; I'm a hip hopper, you know what I
mean? And that's my life—the music and the essence of hip hop."

6/16/03:

I ran into Mekanismn today as I was walking up the stairs at *LJ*; I was
on the staircase going up to 2N, and he was on the staircase coming down
from the third floor. At first, I just peripherally saw a tall guy, and heard
him say "Hi," so I said hi, without really looking. But when we both
reached the landing, he said, "Susan!" and I looked and said,
"Mekanismn!" I hadn't seen him since before Christmas.

Anyway, at some point during our initial chatting in the hall, I of
course said, "Hey, want to be interviewed?" I explained to him what I was
working on, and how I wanted to update the interview of him I had done
before. He said, "Sure. Now?"

Mekanismn is another graduate of *La Juventud* who was in some of
my classes when I taught there full-time. He's a smart guy, creative and
insightful, but his handwriting was always atrocious. In order to be able
to read the lyrics he was constantly writing and occasionally submitting to
the school literary magazine, we found ourselves more than once sitting
in the school library during lunch or after school, him reading his words
out loud while I typed them into the computer, asking questions about
meaning and format as we went along. These moments made me feel
better about not being able to interpret Mekanismn's writing, since there
were often long pauses in his reading while he tried to figure out his own
penmanship.

Like many of The Writers, Mekanismn has an egalitarian nature; his
self-identification as a hip-hopper is both a result and a source of his
respect for people's varying backgrounds and experiences, his instinct
toward thinking the best of people until they give him a reason not to. I
first interviewed him for a paper I was writing on teenagers' ethnoracial
self-perceptions. At the time, he resisted the idea of labeling himself.
Similarly, when I ask him about rapper Eminem's movie *8 Mile*, and
whether he feels that the (White) character in that movie was ultimately
accepted by his (primarily Black) audience because he shared their class
background, thus suggesting that perhaps class trumps race, he calmly but
immediately disagrees: "Hip-hop is not a class, is not a race. Hip-hop
takes anybody. Hip-hop is skill—you gotta have skill. You can be a damn
duck, you know what I mean?"

When we were getting up to leave the office, I asked if he had his
songs recorded. He said yes, and I asked if it would be possible to get a

copy. He smiled and said, "Naw, not yet." I explained that I'm not going to publish his songs if he doesn't want me to, but that it helps me to understand the things he says in the interview if I can look at his current writing. I asked if he had any lyrics written down that I could copy; he said that he had one thing at home, that he actually only had one copy of it, hanging on his wall. He said that he was giving me an important piece of writing, which he was thinking about using as the intro to his CD (he has since given me permission to reproduce these lyrics here).

"Now I Know Why"

Now I know why Common[3] left 'n went to NY/
Cause we don't get no love in the chi[4]/
and on a higher level/
look how the media depict us when we die/
They say that we're crack fiends/
Instead of black kings and queens/
S@#$ we're all human beings/
Though it seems/
That we're becoming desensitized/
the city is so uncivilized/
Look how the crime rise/
They tearing down our high rise/
Destroyin our foundations/
Slowly cuttin off our education/
Like f@#% reparations/
We're all in dyin need/
Becoming last of a dyin breed/
Deprived of our human rights/
I'm sure our people didn't find what's right in the bill of rights/
Why you think our people strike/
Some got struck/
But still they don't give up/
They always get up/
The majority of our populous is fed up/
So now it's time to take our stand/
Aren't you tired of being a troubled man/
They claim our government has our well being in hand/
More like our fate/
The predators is snarlin at our gate/
F#$@ democracy, why should I vote for your mediocre philosophy/
You're just telling lies to me/
Add one spoiled apple to the batch/
And see could you see/
I feel like dead prez/
So lets get free[5]/

PATRICIA

"When I see a plain piece of paper and a pen, it makes me want
to write."

During the winter of 2002/2003, Patricia was in my creative writing class
at *La Juventud*. Patricia was one of a number of African American students who began attending *LJ* as the school was awarded grants from
municipal agencies. Her attendance was spotty; when she did appear several weeks after the New Year, she said that she had been having family
problems since Thanksgiving. She also said, "Susan, I've been writing like
crazy." Although I had known Patricia for a couple of years, I had not
realized how much she wrote. Around school, she was known more as the
girl who walked the halls singing—any time we heard a voice filtering
into the classroom through a closed door, we'd look at each other and say,
"Patricia."

I interviewed Patricia soon after she had moved into her new apartment, a one-bedroom in a primarily Mexican-American neighborhood on
the near-southwest side of Chicago. She had been placed in the apartment
through the Department of Children and Family Services. Arriving there,
I rang the bell and was startled when she yelled down, her head jutting out
from a second floor window: "Hey, Susan. I was looking out for you."

"Hey," I yelled back up.

"My baby's father is coming down to let you in."

When I entered the apartment, Patricia was sitting at a kitchen table
placed against the wall next to the door, both of her children with her. In
the corner, dolls and teddy bears were piled on top of a plastic bin. I started
off asking her if she was currently doing a lot of writing. She said no:

> Right now since, the timing, I have to look after the
> children, now I have two, so, you know, it kind of
> drives me crazy. I don't hardly ever get a chance to do
> anything much as I used to.

SW: A month ago, when you came in you hadn't been at
> school for a while, and you said you had been writing
> like crazy.

Patricia: [I have] a lot of stuff from even a long time ago, I still
> got folders, I got papers, so many papers, all of those
> boxes right there are full of papers [indicating the boxes
> piled on top of each other in the corner next to the
> table].

SW: From how long ago?

Patricia: From like even before when I had her (her daughter
            and oldest child), even before when I had my job and
            stuff, it's like papers, papers, papers.
SW: Do you remember when you started [writing]? Or was
            there something that made you start?
Patricia: I never really thought about that. I had always did
            something else, but I just tried to find time to write. I
            don't know why, but I always did.
SW: In grade school?
Patricia: Yeah, all the time.
SW: Did you get encouragement from family?
Patricia: I was probably writing something *about* them ((soft
            laugh)), but I don't think they encouraged me. It was
            on my own.
SW: Do you remember if there were teachers who encour-
            aged you?
Patricia (sounding surprised): Yeah. A lot of people noticed it,
            like in grade school, that's when we was getting the
            journals, and we had to write in the journals eeeevery
            day, eeeevery day, and that's how—I was just so used to
            writing in the journals, that it kind of clicked, that I . . .
            started to write stuff down.
[At this point, Patricia's four-year-old daughter wanders into the
kitchen.]
Patricia [to daughter]: Come here, let me show you how smart
            she is. Come here. Count up. Count in Spanish (daugh-
            ter counts after a few false starts, in a little girl voice,
            getting them all right except *seis*—Patricia coaches her:
            "*seis*," and the daughter repeats it, then continues
            counting up to *diez*).
SW: Wow! Where'd you learn that?
Patricia [to daughter]: And ABCs.
Daughter: What?
Patricia: Tell her your ABCs.
Daughter sings the ABCs.
[After her daughter leaves, we return to our conversation.]
SW: Did you grow up with your parents?
Patricia: Mmhmmm. I never grew up with my father, but my
            mom.
SW: Brothers and sisters?
Patricia: Mmhmm. Three of each, three brothers and three sisters.
SW: Were there books and magazines in your house?

Patricia: Books. Kids' books. All *Cat in the Hat*. Those were like my favorite books. *Green Eggs and Ham* . . .

SW: Tell me a little about your history . . .

Patricia: I grew up on the west side of Chicago all my life . . . [It was] me, my sister, and my brother, as far as I remember . . . 'Cause after awhile, when we got older—around ten or eleven—we all got separated 'cause we got tooken from my mom . . . so I didn't really get much time to spend with my younger brothers and sisters, like I did with my older sister and my younger brother.

SW: Why did you get taken away?

Patricia: They call it neglect, when your mother do drugs, but there wasn't ever really no neglect. Not to me . . . 'cause my mother was always there. Even though that was her way of hiding her pain or however she felt, that was her way of doing what she had to do, but it never took away from us. You know, it never took *her* away from us. But, that's what she chose to do.

"The Rainbow"

When I was young
only about 10 yrs old
I remember that over the rainbow
Sat a big pot of gold
I would always dream and stare
That one day I would find
a way to get over there.

Some days the sun will shine
and it will rain all day
and the only thing I would do is pray
pray that we could have that
big pot of gold.

So we would never have to
worry about our clothes getting old
we would never have to worry about
having no food to eat
or raggedy shoes on our feet

I still dream
as I lay on the floor
that one day I'll get
across that rainbow.

ROBBIE

"I just said, 'You know what? If I can do all this martial arts, and I can think this much, how about I just write something down? Let me see what I'm gonna say.'"

10/23/02:

Driving in to *LJ* this afternoon, looking to my left on the boulevard at a red light, I saw a group of seven or eight guys standing on the steps of a house. I realized that one of them was Robbie; his hair—dark, thick, floppy, and longer every time I see him—makes him identifiable from far away. The principal came into class after it had started, asking how many students I was missing. I got my attendance book, and we went down the list of names together, him telling me who was absent and who seemed to have cut. When we got to Robbie, he said, "Write him down as a cut. He's in my office, but you can put him as absent." I was disappointed because Robbie had said he was bringing in his big stack of poems today for me to read and copy.

Halfway through the class, Robbie walked in smiling and sat down next to Jane and Jonathan. "I brought the poems," he said. He reached into his bag and pulled out a sloppy pile of mostly blue-lined notebook paper with ragged, hanging edges. I took the stack and started leafing through it, pulling out the occasional small piece of paper. Pointing to one of these, he said, "That's the first poem I wrote, the one I told you about. I just woke up and wrote it down." I asked when he wrote it. He thought for a moment, then said "Eighth grade." Looking at the pile I was holding, Jonathan said to Robbie, "Did you write all of that?" Jane said to me, "Can I read them after you're done?" Looking at Robbie for approval, I said, "Is it okay if I hold onto them and give them back to you on Friday?" He said yes, and Jane stretched her hand toward me, saying, "Oh, well then let me read them now." I looked at Robbie and asked, "Is that okay?" "Yeah, I show her my poems."

Apparently, he shares them with several friends at school. I came across Robbie and another student, Juan, hanging out in a teacher's class during lunch one day. When Juan mentioned that he did some rap freestyling, I asked if I could interview him. He demurred, saying he's not a writer. I tried to convince him by pointing to Robbie, who was standing to my side, and saying, "Robbie's done it. It's not so scary." Robbie nodded, and Juan replied, "Yeah, but Robbie's stuff is deep."

Back in the writing workshop, near the end of the period, Robbie came over and sat next to me. He started going through the pile as I held it, pulling out a piece of paper here and there, and explaining some specific thing about the poems. He came across a small, folded paper, grabbed it and stuffed it in his back pants pocket: "That's not a poem. That's a letter to my girlfriend," he explained, sounding embarrassed. He saw another small piece of paper; it, too, disappeared into his pocket: "That's some lyrics." On another piece, he pointed out a couple of lines written in black ink on the back: "This is a quote that I wrote. I had this daily planner with quotes on every day, from Mark Twain and people. So I wrote this."

I asked how his parents felt about his writing, and if he showed it to them. "To my dad, yeah. My mom only speaks Spanish. She can understand some English, but if I show them to her, she'll say, 'Well, it looks like you wrote a lot, so that's good.' My dad says, 'I've listened to a lot of music, and this sounds like the lyrics to those songs . . . '" I asked if his parents write: "My dad used to read to me a lot when I was a kid, a lot of horror stories." I asked where the darkness in his writing comes from: "We used to watch a lot of horror movies . . . "

He tries to teach us wrong from what's right
He tries to bring us into the brightest of light
Resist the sin only then can be saved,
fall into sin forever engraved.
These rules were made for us to live.
Human population we have all to give.
For all that look down for once look up.
Only God we trust until burned to dust.
Fate falls, a random pick.
Heaven performs there little tricks.
He strives for good never bad,
now let's see what drove him mad.
He showed us confusion and gave us pain.
Things he did were much insane.
Starvation began to those who lie.
Adam and Eve were left to die.
2nd chances not given for human beginners,
Now only thing left is sinner and sinners.
All can contribute to a human's pain in life,
from the past we see it's not as straight as we like.

TeTe

"I've been writing since, like, forever."

At fifteen, TeTe is the youngest of the four Maniacs in this study. She is also the sister of Jig and Crazy, and shares their good nature, intelligence, and love of music and writing:

> I always wrote poetry, 'cause I get that from my momma. But when I heard my brothers rapping—and I always knew how to rap—but I heard my brothers rapping, I'm like, 'I could do that.' So I wrote my stuff down, like yeah, okay. [Now] I think I could be like equal to my brother Crazy, on my best day. ((Laughs, then points to Jig)) [But] I can't touch him.

TeTe is very conscious of the sibling hierarchy; she tells me at one point that she feels like her two older brothers got the best of the intelligence and talent, and she got stuck with the leftovers. Whenever she says things like this, though, it's with a mixture of ruefulness and humor. It's true that she doesn't earn the straight As that have become the norm for Jig and Crazy:

> SW: Do you do well [in school]?
> TeTe: I do well in English classes.
>   ((Jig laughs))
> TeTe: Math?? Math??
> SW: You're like me.
> TeTe: On the other hand, I'd rather have someone do my home-
>   work, 'cause he's [indicates Jig] like a calculator. Any prob-
>   lem, anything, he'll know. I don't know how.

As she says this, I wonder to what extent she simply hasn't felt the need to master as much on her own precisely because she's got two over-achieving brothers at home to help her out. Yet TeTe's no slouch: she writes poetry and prose, and is a full member of the Maniacs with her own very distinct persona (we'll hear more about this in upcoming chapters). She proudly tells stories of having surprised her brothers and their friends with her wordplay. She also has her own singing group, consisting of herself and a couple of girlfriends. Within this group, she is able to take on the leadership role that Jig embodies for her and Crazy.

TeTe's family seems to have given her a balance of protection and freedom. When I pick her and Jig up to see a documentary on a San

Francisco rapper playing at a small, north side gallery, she is dressed in a clingy, one-sleeved red top and tight jeans. I am chatting with her father when she walks into the living room; he immediately comments on her clothing—he seems not so much worried about her being too sexy as about her being possibly overdressed for the occasion. He looks to me, and I assure him that she'll fit in fine. While I continue waiting for Jig, TeTe runs outside; when her brother finally appears, he and I have to drive down the block after her—we find her walking with a guy about a block and half down from their house.

Another day, while I am once again at the siblings' house, someone jokingly makes reference to TeTe's "street pharmacist" boyfriend. I am taken aback, and don't know whether they are being serious or not. "Street pharmacist" is slang for "drug dealer," and my experience with this family had led me to believe that they have avoided drug use and abuse. This is one of a million lessons I learn during the course of my research—distinctions are never clear, especially for youth living in low-income urban neighborhoods where drugs and crime may coexist with deep religious faith and strong familial bonds. This street pharmacist, I learn later, is a young man TeTe has known since both were young children. They will, in fact, later plan to move together to Arizona with TeTe's mother, at least partly so that he can break out of the lifestyle he has developed in Chicago.

At the time of this research, TeTe is on the cusp between girl and young woman. She plays with sexuality in her lyrics and makes important decisions about her life at the same time that she participates in conversations with fans on the website of B2K, a popular boy band of attractive, carefully packaged teenagers created just for girls like her.

(from the Alicia Keys website message boards)
***Te-Te (Of the Maniacs)*—06:50pm Jun 10, 2003 EST**

Ayo, if anybody in Chicago readin' this, have y'all noticed since last Monday it done been raining non stop except for today?

have u noticed since last monday night
it don been a cold and rainy and horrible sight
another 1 of our good soldiers fell
4 shots to the dome but he ain't goin to hell
he done did his thang on earth
and then some niggas wanna kill em wut's the worth?
now he ain't even gon be able to see his first child's birth
god chose to take another good 1 from us
but I guess juan was too good to be walkin among us
he the only 1 in school that was a faithful friend
and fa sho he was a good friend down to the end
I know he probably like "dayum te can rap and I never got her #" and then he snaps
the last words that we spoke was about prom pictures
I was like u give me a picture I give u my number and maybe we could kick it this summer
he was like aight I got u next week
this was the day I would have the picture
but instead I got a obituary with a written scripture
it said he died 18 about to graduate
goin to college but them niggas had to hate
see this shit happened cuz of some shit last year
juan whooped some nigga ass till his death came near
but that nigga was in juan's face so he shoulda took his whoopin like a man then gave 'em some space
but that's the thing juan wouldn't kill nobody
before death came he left dude body
and now chicken heads tryin to say its juan's fault
aight let a bitch say that shit to me again and when I kick u down the stairs it'll be yo fault
cuz i warned u first off and u ain't have to go that far with it
and for talkin shit
but fuck these ho ass niggas and bitches fuck flowers and shyt in ya casket u gettin my digits
R.I.P
Juan
B.K.A
Pretty Poke
A.K.A
Pokey

2

"You Never Let Me Speak"

POWER, LANGUAGE, AND LEARNING

> **"Understand!?"**
> *by Dave*
>
> I've got words to say
> certain thoughts I'm dying to utter
> coming raw from my mind's gutter
> I've held back for too long
> and you're gonna hear me out
> even if you think I'm wrong
> don't turn your back on me
> don't roll your eyes and wave your hand
> I won't be ignored understand!?
> you never let me speak
> but now it's my turn
> and my momentum won't be beat
> my voice will ring in your ears
> my rage will reflect in my tears
> one moment to exhale emotions of many years
> don't turn your back on me
> don't roll your eyes or wave your hand
> I won't be ignored understand!?

— —

It takes an extraordinarily strong character and perseverance to counter the structure of visibility and invisibility, to see oneself as a writer and one's writing as worthy when few of the social institutions in society support such a view (and indeed may actively support just the opposite). (Sheridan et al., 2000, 7)

— —

This chapter is about the sociocultural forces that make literacy events come to *mean* in different ways. Those forces include the ones that make youths' literacy practices seem marginal to many people, even though these ways with words (Heath, 1983) are, in the contexts of the young people's experiences, vitally important and legitimate. Sociocultural conflicts play out in the literacy arena from the smallest communicative element—the word—to the most complex pieces of literature. Therefore, we cannot talk about the writing of marginalized youth without talking about the language practices that comprise it; as Gee notes, "in order to define 'literacy' adequately we must first discuss a few other concepts which are commonly misconstrued. One of these is language" (1996, 124). The writers in this study often use negatively marked dialects in their speech and writing—that is to say, dialects that depart from the standardized English norm and that have historically been identified in the public mind with lack of intelligence, education, and—quite literally—class. The Writers also focus on topics that cause concern in adults—sexuality, violence, incarceration. There is ongoing debate over the role that commercial culture, in the forms of popular music, television, and film, plays in attracting young people to risky practices that—the argument goes—they would otherwise avoid because of the positive influences of family and institutionalized programs. Yet while this chicken-egg debate goes on in the media, courtrooms, and legislatures, for each of The Writers, such topics are the stuff of everyday life, and writing about them is a powerful way of working through difficult experiences.

Marginalized children are often raised within speech communities whose ways with words are similarly marginalized. When there is a fundamental ideological conflict between the languages and literacies that are valued at home and those that are required by school, confusion, resentment, and/or resistance are inevitable. John Ogbu (1991) makes an important distinction between voluntary and involuntary minorities in terms of attitudes toward such sociocultural conflicts, noting that individuals and groups who have chosen to come to the United States and who view their situation in the U.S. in relation to a less desirable situation in their country of origin tend to accept such conflicts as a normal part of the immigrant experience, and accept the push toward assimilation relatively uncritically. Involuntary minorities have a more complicated relationship with the dominant culture. These groups include descendents of slaves, for example, or those of Mexican origin whose forebears' lands were taken over by encroaching European, then American, colonists. For a historically oppressed group to take on the language, values, and prac-

tices of a system perceived as oppressive creates powerful emotional, rela-
tional, and ideological conflicts. "Used to speak the King's English, but
caught a rash on my lips/So now my chat just like dis . . .", rapper Mos
Def (1999c) rhymes, stretching the word "English" into three syllables—
"Eng-a-lish"—in mock over-formality before flipping to the vernacular of
"chat" and "dis," thus embodying in word choice and pronunciation the
resistant linguistic choices so many Americans make.

In terms of language and literacy, a central area where this ideological
conflict is manifested is dialect:

> Let us assume for the moment that all children are loyal to their
> native vernacular, while schools simultaneously advocate mastery
> of the standard dialect [SE, or Standard English], as they must.
> The very linguistic allegiance that enhances educational
> prospects for native standard speakers stands in opposition to the
> success of nonstandard speakers. While educators recognize the
> vital role of SE to future success, the demands in out-of-school
> contexts may be quite different . . . (Baugh, 1999, 67–68)

In other words, a conscious resistance to academic language can lead to
"covert prestige" (Baugh 1999, 70) on the streets, where standardized
speech may be viewed as White, as (for males) feminine, as racist, or as
not delivering on its social and economic promises.

This chapter offers an overview of public sphere discourses and
debates on U.S. language and youth practices and policy over the last
decade, focusing specifically on the practices of African-Americans and
Latinos as these are the ethnoracial categories represented by The Writers. We will revisit the Ebonics controversy of 1996/1997 and analyze
media representations of young rappers and poets in order to make
explicit the ideologies that drive the public conversation on marginalized
youth and their literacy practices. We will also touch briefly on representations of African-American orality in order to demonstrate how the literacy practices of people like Jig, Crazy, Mekanismn, TeTe, and Patricia
(the five African-American Writers) have tended to be oversimplified and
misrepresented, narrativized in ways that obscure the complexity of their
lived histories. Finally, I will survey the specific circumstances in which
many urban, ethnoracially and economically marginalized young people
live. As you read this book, you will encounter youth who have grown up
in foster care, who have been incarcerated, who are teen parents, who
have dropped out of high school (sometimes more than once). Through
an exploration of these issues, I hope to demonstrate the insidious
pressures that work to discourage young people from doing the kind of

writing that makes sense to them, that grants them considerable rewards, and from which they learn because they *want* to.

THE EBONICS DEBATE

> A lot of cultures need to understand . . . that if you oppressed us and you kept us in this condition and took our language from us then we would develop a language to communicate with each other.
>
> Professor Griff of Public Enemy (qtd. in Toop, 2000, 210)

— —

7/26/03 Instant Messenger conversation between Jig and me:

sueweinst says:
> So I'm working on Chapter One . . . Trying to write about the Ebonics debate back in 1996–7. I'm going to write about the various reactions to it, and what that says about the country's attitudes towards the people who speak it.

Jig says:
> yeah they think we're dumb

sueweinst says:
> Not everyone. The linguists all sided with the school board, which was recognizing it as a language.

Jig says:
> that's interesting, but technically speaking, it is a language, an ever evolving one since new words are made everyday, and old ones thrown out, but it is a language, and can be hard to learn for some people

Jig says:
> i knew i was Bi-lingual

— —

Jig's response above brims with affective signals. He owns the language under discussion immediately, as signaled by the use of "we" to reference Ebonics speakers. His response to the mention of attitudes toward Ebonics speakers is that "they think we're dumb." The "they" is necessarily nebulous, and suggests that this young Black man, at least, experiences negative judgments based on language as coming from many directions. Yet he turns the tables on "them" by taking on an official-sounding, scholarly tone to claim legitimacy for the language he speaks, and then ends by wryly intoning a concept that has been used more than once in pointing up the irony inherent in educators' and others' devaluing of Ebonics—that is, that bilingualism or multilingualism are valued in the United States as long as the non-English languages spoken carry comparable cultural capital to English. Yet native dialects are regularly devalued, seen as sometimes almost pathological deviations from the standard. Even completely distinct languages are valued differently depending on who speaks them. Spanish is a fixture of most foreign language curricula in American schools, yet when Latin American immigrants speak it, it transforms into a problem, raising suspicions of illegality and poverty.

Given such attitudes, one can even now almost hear the jaws hitting the floor when it was suggested that African-Americans spoke another *language*, and that a school district wanted to *pay* to train teachers in Ebonics so that they could provide bilingual services to their Black students—it being hard enough to find districts where sufficient funding and support existed for young speakers of languages completely distinct from English. The reaction to the Oakland Unified School District's (OUSD) December 1996 resolution was predictably loud and emotional. On January 23, 1997, members of the U.S. Senate Appropriations Subcommittee debated the advisability of funding programs like the one the OUSD proposed. Senator Lauch Faircloth (R-North Carolina) said:

> I think Ebonics is absurd. This is a political correctness that simply has gone out of control . . . Now I'm very much aware that teaching children in schools in the inner cities and in poor neighborhoods all over the country, rural or inner city, has never been easy, and it never will be. But rather than trying to lower the academic standards, we should try some of the old-fashioned remedies that I think would still work. Nobody should be passed from grade to grade unless they can master the basic three R's of reading, writing, and arithmetic. (qtd. in Holman, 1997 [online])

The argument of radio talk show host Armstrong Williams, who spoke at the committee hearing, rested on the characterization of Ebonics as simply bad English:

> A teacher would not teach mathematics by trying to show that he or she could make mistakes in addition or subtraction. Must one's senators have to smoke marijuana to be able to relate to teen-age drug addiction? Should they smoke marijuana in order

to teach them a better way? Definitely not. And the same is true
with language. (qtd. in Holman, 1997 [online])

Educators found themselves conflicted on the issue. An online conversation among members of the National Council of Teachers of English's Assembly for the Teaching of English Grammar[1] displayed some of
their concerns. Larry Beason, Director of English Composition at Eastern Washington University, wrote:

> I'm sure the move in Oakland was well intended, but I cannot
> believe that it will help students—esp. the minorities whom it
> was intended to help—nor does the rationale represent current
> thinking on what is a langauge [sic]. What bugs me is that the
> ultra-conservatives are having a field day with this one, and I find
> myself agreeing w/ their stance but not their tone, rhetoric, or
> reasons. (23 Dec. 1996)

Another educator on the site, Bill Murdick, reluctantly supported the
OUSD: "Whatever one does in these cases, it cannot be worse than what
is being done in the traditional classroom. I don't like the idea of makeing
[sic] dialect differences 'official,' but if using a concept like 'ebonics' can
release students from frustration and lead them to try out reading and
writing, I would support it" (24 Dec. 1996).

All of these responses demonstrate the extent to which conversations
about marginalized language systems are primarily ideological, rather
than scholarly or practical, in nature. Senator Faircloth calls on the popular bugaboo of political correctness to discredit the Ebonics resolution.
Political correctness is a term that has been used since the 1980s, usually
hurled at liberals by conservatives as a way of rendering any attempt at
recognizing and respecting difference ridiculous. It is dismissal by association, rather than by reasoned argument. Senator Faircloth then dismisses Oakland's attempt to try something new because, as he says
somewhat ominously, "it never will be" easy to educate the children of the
poor. His solution? Keep doing what's always been done, and punish the
students by holding them back if these strategies don't work. Everything
in Faircloth's statement resists change, especially (I would argue) change
in the conditions that lead to academic failure.

Radio host Williams' remarks are utterly transparent: Ebonics is not
only bad English; it is akin to making mistakes in math or even to smok-
ing marijuana—suggesting that the language that many Black school-
children speak is both unintellectual and, if I read Williams' tone
correctly, morally degenerate.

Professor Beason's comments are certainly more measured, his tone in disagreeing with the Oakland School Board regretful. But politics does indeed make strange bedfellows—he feels sullied by his agreement with "ultra-conservatives," yet his rational-sounding argument (that the resolution "does not represent current thinking" on what makes a language) seems less rational when read in the light of both the Linguistic Society of America's (LSA) and the Center for Applied Linguistics's (CAL) contemporaneous statements in support of the OUSB's action:

> Much of the criticism of Oakland's policy has viewed the students' language as "bad," "ungrammatical," or "malformed," essentially a collection of language mistakes rather than a system that differs in certain features from other dialects. This opinion is not supported by linguistic research, and it misses an important educational point: students' implicit linguistic knowledge of their own dialect can be used for contrasting features of their dialect with features of the standard dialect which the schools want to teach them . . . Comparing the facts about language variation from dialect to dialect with social attitudes about dialects both fascinates and outrages students. It also provides a rational basis for dialect learning. (Linguistic Society of America)

Finally, educator Bill Murdick says that he doesn't "like the idea of making dialect differences official." I sympathize with this point—the compartmentalizing of dialects, and by extension of their speakers, could potentially be a step backward in terms of ongoing efforts at integration and cross-cultural understanding. Yet Murdick's response demonstrates that supporters of the Oakland resolution, too, speak from ideology— Murdick's concern seems to be not ultimately about the dialects themselves as much as about the effect such a move will have on relationships among diverse individuals and groups.

The two educators quoted above have reservations about the Ebonics-as-language argument that the Oakland school board included in its resolution. The influential linguistic ethnographer William Labov says that this is common of many people who are sympathetic to the plight of marginalized kids in bad schools: "They reject the view that social and educational failure in the inner city is the result of laziness or the intellectual inferiority of African Americans. Yet among these people of good will, many are ready to apply these same labels to the language of African Americans" (in Baugh, 1999, ix).

Given the content of responses to the Oakland resolution, one might wish that its authors had substituted the term *dialect* for *language*, thus focusing the attention where it belongs—on the difficulties AAVE speakers have in classrooms where only standardized English is validated—and away from the less significant (for classroom teachers) question of whether Ebonics is indeed a separate language. Yet the Oakland Board's claim for full language status for AAVE was critical to the resolution, functioning as either a pragmatic or a cynical move (depending on one's own stance) to create the basis for demanding local and federal Title VII bilingual education funds for the district's schools.

While the Oakland resolution is ten years old at the time of this writing, the controversy surrounding it remains a productive area of study. Baugh (1999) notes that "the Ebonics controversy . . . serves greatly to amplify concerns regarding African American miseducation" (41). Baugh is ultimately critical of the Oakland resolution, both because of its essentializing connections between language and race and because of its implied characterization of AAVE "as a barrier to academic success" in and of itself, rather than because of existing "linguistic prejudice" (54). However, he acknowledges that the resolution was motivated by "laudable educational intentions" (58), and he echoes Labov's position regarding the ideological roots of the Oakland controversy: "Although we may believe that our misconceptions about AAVE are linguistic, they are fundamentally racial and lead even scientists and scholars to grossly erroneous conclusions about the intelligence of black people" (6). In a theme that will be repeated throughout this book, the Ebonics debate demonstrates that real changes in the quality of education for marginalized youth absolutely require changes in teacher preparation and professional development in order to develop among all educators (not just English Language Arts teachers) a clear understanding of and respect for students' home languages, dialects, and cultures. There has certainly been some movement in this direction in the years since the Oakland resolution, but too many teachers, administrators, and policy makers still believe that the ways with words of marginalized populations are simply wrong, and therefore cannot possibly hold any potential for productive incorporation into the classroom.

THE MYTH OF ORALITY

While African-American-identified speech patterns have been attacked in various ways, as discussed above, one element—orality—has been a traditional subject of celebration. Much has been written about the ways that West African oral forms were interwoven with new world experiences of slavery, dispersion, and Christianity, resulting in slave songs and narratives, in the rich oratory of the Black church, in the competitive insult play of the Dozens, in the elaborate folk narratives known as toasts, and in young girls' playground rhymes. Yet this emphasis on orality in African-American culture serves a less obvious purpose, implying that written literacy is not a central feature of the culture.

McHenry and Heath (1994) identify two central reasons for this biased representation. One is class-based: "Especially since the 1960s, it has been more fashionable to valorize poverty than to detail the contributions of middle- and upper-class African Americans" (261), and when language researchers focus on poor populations, they are likely to find less or less-effective formal education, and therefore less-developed abilities with writing. When one broadens the focus to include the middle- and upper-classes, it becomes clear that African-Americans have been forming and participating in literary societies, and publishing and contributing to newspapers, journals, and literary magazines, since at least the early 1800s (McHenry and Heath, 1994, 262). Sometimes, though, keeping the lens narrow can be useful:

> The denial or omission of these [literate] events and organizations from both scholarly treatment and pedagogical background for presentation of literary works by African Americans has served academic culture by allowing the distancing and objectifying of African Americans while reserving designations such as "literate" for the "dominant" culture. The focus on African American orality has thus often implied an absence of reason and permanence, in contrast to the presence of these properties within literacy and particularly habits that surround the reading and writing of literature. (McHenry and Heath, 1994, 263)

McHenry and Heath argue that some of the most celebrated African-American oral forms, such as religious oratory, "are often deeply based in written preparations and source texts," and are often not only written but "*re*written (using notes written before performance as well as the experience of the oral delivery)" (264, italics in original). Even purely oral performances borrow "numerous rhetorical and lexical choices . . . from written materials [which] stabilize the verbal art of the oral text" (264; see also Heath, 1983, 201–211).

For McHenry and Heath, the goal is to explode a limited and limiting definition of African American literacies, and to introduce middle- and upper-class African-American discourses into the picture that scholars continue to construct of these practices. For African-Americans, as for others, reading, writing, and oral performance are inextricably intertwined. One thing that the present study will demonstrate is that this is no less true for working-class African-Americans than for the middle class.

McHenry and Heath challenge the popular view of African-American literacy as primarily oral by arguing that this view must change when middle- and upper-class experiences are added to the picture; I value their correction to traditional scholarship, and now make another move with this new perspective in hand, back to the working classes, so that we can reconsider the extent to which the primarily oral nature of *their* literacy practices has also been overstated. The writing of TeTe, Jig, Crazy, and Mekanismn provides an ideal set of practices to study in this vein. They participate in a Discourse—rap—in which the final product is presented orally, and in which the physical and vocal elements of oral performance are integral to the meaning, quality, and reception of the text. Yet there is hidden work that leads to that product involving intensive writing, often in more than one medium (pen and paper, word processing programs, online message boards). If the myth of African-American orality leads to lowered expectations or to negative assumptions about young Black men's and women's writing abilities, then this book challenges that myth with concrete evidence of such youths' passion for written composition.

ESL, BILINGUAL, OR IMMERSION?

> I remember being caught speaking Spanish at recess—that was good for three licks on the knuckles with a sharp ruler. I remember being sent to the corner of the classroom for "talking back" to the Anglo teacher when all I was trying to do was tell her how to pronounce my name. "If you want to be American, speak 'American.' If you don't like it, go back to Mexico where you belong."
>
> —Gloria Anzaldua, *Borderlands* (1987)

The Ebonics controversy revealed attitudes surrounding *native* English speakers whose particular code is negatively marked in terms of intelligence, economic position and potential, and, of course, race. Dialogue over the best way of assimilating non-native English speakers uncovers another facet of U.S. language ideology. While speakers of African-American Vernacular English can and have made arguments that using standardized English is a politically capitulative move through which they agree to take on the voice (verbal and ideological) of their historical oppressors, sheer practicality suggests that new immigrants learn English so they can effectively navigate the public interactions that make up so much of everyday life. Of The Writers, Robbie, Marta, José, and Dave come from Spanish-speaking families; Robbie, Marta, and José are of

Mexican heritage, while Dave's parents both emigrated from Peru to the U.S. While these youths' facility with both English and Spanish varies, a brief look at U.S. educational policy concerning non-native speakers is relevant given my general argument that official language policy is primarily about ideological stances toward *speakers*. Thus, whether or not any of these four writers went through one of the second-language educational models described below, the attitudes revealed toward non-native speakers by such models are ones that these writers are subject to.

The debate surrounding the education of non-native speakers centers on how English is best *taught* and *learned*. It may seem redundant to use both of these verbs, but one of the complexities of this issue is that, too often, opinions over how to most effectively teach and learn English do not intersect. This gap offers a powerful example of the extent to which ideology can drive research, rather than the other way around, and it complicates the adoption of any of the three basic models for teaching English to non-native speakers—bilingual education, English as a Second Language (ESL) instruction, and English immersion—even as each of the three models can point to successes and failures, to supportive and critical "empirical" research findings.

1. English as a Second Language (ESL)

The ESL approach is the middle path in this trio, incorporating a little of each of the others in its pedagogy. In one ESL model, students attend some mainstream classes with their English-speaking peers—generally classes where a lack of English is not seen as a major drawback, like physical education or art. These students also spend part of the school day in a separate classroom where, as the term implies, English is taught as a second (or other) language, the way that English-speaking students might study Spanish—through drill, memorization, and conversational practice using short, preconstructed dialogues.

In the ESL model, students spend some part of their day interacting with English-speaking peers, something that is generally agreed to be a necessity for the effective learning of a language. They may get more individualized attention in the sometimes smaller ESL classes than they would in a regular classroom. And, for communities that have diverse language populations, comprising, say, recent immigrants from Latin America, Southeast Asia, Eastern Europe, and/or the Middle East, ESL is the only practical solution. A school can realistically hire one, or even several, English-speaking instructors with ESL training, whereas the cost to hire instructors who speak each of the languages represented in the school would quickly become prohibitive, and create impossible demands on physical space.

There are, however, two major arguments against ESL. First, the approach does not consistently result in linguistic fluency. Second, and perhaps more persuasively, students who are already at an academic disadvantage because of the disruption that immigration has caused in their education often fall further behind when their classes focus primarily on the learning of English, rather than on the academic subjects being taught to their English-speaking peers—social studies, science, literature, and the like. This lack of content-area instruction can effectively ensure that young people already marginalized by their immigrant and linguistic status are further disadvantaged by a lack of academic preparation.

2. Bilingual Education

Bilingual education developed as a more equitable response to the drawbacks of ESL instruction. Students would be taught by instructors who spoke both English and the students' first language, and they would study content in *both* languages, learning English as part of the process of learning history, math, science, etc. This approach demonstrates a respect for the child's home language and a recognition of the emotional and adaptive benefits of making home languages an accepted part of the school setting. It also has a practical side: with increased globalization, it is difficult to deny the benefits of bi- and even multilingualism. The student whose education simultaneously develops her abilities in two languages is actually at an advantage in this scenario over her monolingual English-speaking peers.

Unfortunately, like so much educational policy, bilingual education has rarely been implemented in ways that allow students to reap its full hypothetical benefits. Studies show that children may need up to six years of either ESL or bilingual education before they can be effectively integrated into English-only classrooms without damage to their academic development. Yet many programs last for only one or two years. Students who come out of such truncated programs into mainstream classrooms are then blamed for their inability to keep up; they effectively take the fall for poor programmatic implementation. This individual blaming both reflects and reinforces notions of individual responsibility for achievement that are foundational to U.S. ideology, veiling structural inadequacy and turning dissatisfaction inward toward one's self, family, and community, rather than outward toward an educational structure that handicaps non-native speakers.

3. Immersion

> The first day of school said a lot about my scholastic life to come.
> I was taken to a teacher who didn't know what to do with me. . .
>
> After some more paperwork, I was taken to another class.
> This time the teacher appeared nicer, but distracted. She got the
> word about my language problem.
>
> "Okay, why don't you sit here in the back of the class," she
> said. "Play with some blocks until we figure out how to get you
> more involved."
>
> It took her most of that year to figure this out. I just stayed
> in the back of the class, building blocks. It got so every morning I
> would put my lunch and coat away, and walk to my corner where
> I stayed the whole day long. It forced me to be more withdrawn.
> It got so bad, I didn't even tell anybody when I had to go to the
> bathroom. I did it in my pants. Soon I stunk back there in the
> corner and the rest of the kids screamed out a chorus of "P.U.!"
> resulting in my being sent to the office or back home.
>
> —Luis Rodriguez, *Always Running* (1993, 26–27)

While the English-only movement in its current form is a fairly recent phenomenon, assimilation through English-language immersion in the classroom is not. In fact, the two previously outlined models—ESL and bilingual instruction—grew out of a recognition of the academic and psychological harm done to immigrant children through English immersion. Luis Rodriguez's memories of his first days in school echo those of many others who, as small children, were forced to either sink or swim. Even those who claim that immersion is the only way to go, such as the author Richard Rodriguez in his book *Hunger of Memory* (1982), reveal such visceral pain, identity conflict, and cultural alienation in their stories that the overt argument for immersion is, for many readers, overpowered by the cries of the subtextual subject.

The English-immersion model is the most overtly ideological of the three approaches to instruction of non-native speakers. It relies on a strict "us-and-them" view, as in, "*They* came to *our* country, so *they* should speak *our* language." It is xenophobic and nationalistic, requiring as it does full capitulation to the language and ideologies of the adopted nation and a complete dismissal of the possible social value of diversity and difference.

Despite the anecdotal arguments for immersion, the strongest argument against it is that it is simply poor pedagogy: "Auerbach [1993] maintains that the exclusive use of English in the classroom results in nonparticipation by students, language shock, dropping out, frustration, and inability to build on existing L1 [first-language] literacy skills" (Valdes, 2001, 157–158). Auerbach echoes the dynamics of the Ebonics debate when he says:

> Despite the fact that use or prohibition of the L1 is often framed in purely pedagogical terms, clearly it is also an ideological issue. Ironically, often the very people who argue vehemently against the English-Only movement on a societal level insist on the exclusive use of English at the classroom level. (qtd. in Valdes, 2001, 157–158)

There is no question that young non-native speakers of English should learn the standardized dialect of the society in which they live—in fact, like other young people, English learners often pick up not only the public standard, but also the dialects used in their neighborhoods and those used in popular media. But the leap from recognizing the need for such youth to learn standardized English to the argument that the only way to do it is to put them in a situation where they can neither speak nor understand is counter-intuitive. Championing an approach that doesn't work is an ideological, not an educational, move that once again reveals stances toward these youths, their cultures, and their place in U.S. society.

Each of The Writers, like all of us, speaks in a number of registers and dialect varieties. While this book is not focused on dialect usage per se, in daily practice youth whose everyday speech features elements that are linked in the public mind to specific economic, national, and ethno-racial categories are often judged based on that language in ways that close off the possibility that such youth have anything of value to say, let alone a real talent for imaginative verbal composition. As Jig says at the beginning of this section, many of those with cultural capital hear the speech of him and others like him and automatically "think we're dumb." Thus, valuing such youth requires that adults examine their own linguistic biases and open themselves to the possibility that there are alternative ways to hear the voices around them.

TO BE YOUNG AND OF COLOR IN THE U.S.A.

As indicated in the Introduction, most of The Writers have dealt with difficult, sometimes painful, challenges in the course of their lives. I didn't purposely look for youth coming out of such circumstances—the fact that in this sample of nine there are experiences of foster care, arrest and imprisonment, dropping out of school, and teenage parenthood is unfortunately unsurprising, given the social and economic realities of life on the south and west sides of Chicago. These experiences become the fodder for The Writers' poetry, prose, and lyrics; they also create in these youth particular stances toward and interpretations of their society. The mantra of personal responsibility is intoned regularly in graduation speeches, newspaper editorials, classroom readings—even in the movies and music specifically targeted at young people (as will be seen in more detail in Chapter Four). The public gaze bears down upon youth like The Writers, too often judging and blaming them for situations that stem in many cases from earliest childhood, long before anyone could reasonably suggest that they would have the agency to change their situations. Through their writing, though, The Writers talk back. To understand what their words mean and where they come from, then, it is important for readers to have a basic knowledge of the social climate in which The Writers live.

As previously mentioned, Patricia, Robbie, Crazy, Mekanismn, José, and Marta all attended an alternative high school for students who had dropped out or been kicked out of the public schools. They returned to school for various reasons, but several continued to struggle with attendance and academic motivation. These six young people are much like their peers around the country: according to the 2000 U.S. Census, 6.9 percent of White youth were school dropouts in 2000, compared to 13.1 percent of Black youth and a staggering 27.8 percent of Hispanic youth. In Chicago, according to data compiled in 2004, the balance is somewhat different, but no less troubling. While Hispanic/Latino youth have the highest dropout rate nationwide, in Chicago, African-American youth take that position. Still, though, both groups lag behind White and Asian students in terms of high school completion:

- Among boys, only 39 percent of African-Americans graduated by age 19, compared to 51 percent of Latinos, 58 percent of Whites, and 76 percent of Asians.
- Graduation rates among girls were much higher, but still skewed: 57 percent of African-Americans graduated by age 19, 65 percent of Latinas, 71 percent of Whites, and 85 percent of Asians.
- Over the past seven years [as of 2004], African-American students showed less improvement in graduation and dropout rates than other groups of students. Consistent with Chicago's racially segregated neighborhoods, the report finds that communities on Chicago's mostly African-American South Side saw less improvement in graduation and dropout rates than did North Side communities. (Allensworth, 2005, 3)

The Illinois Department of Child and Family Services (DCFS) is another institution that plays a major role in the lives of poor children of color. Among The Writers, both José and Patricia were wards of the state for several years; during the time I conducted this research, both were in the process of being emancipated from the state foster care system, with Patricia receiving subsidized housing for her and her two (soon to be three) children. José's removal from his birth family was due to severe physical abuse, while Patricia's mother was addicted to drugs. Again, and unfortunately, Patricia and José fit the profile of state wards. "Children of color are disproportionately represented in the child welfare system," youth worker Mark Courtney notes (2004, 10), while former Illinois DCFS director Jess McDonald says that "50 percent of abuse and neglect reports come from a small number of areas that are high in poverty and unemployment and have been abandoned by most other public-sector agencies" (in Poertner, 2004, 7).

While the reality of dropout rates and other social statistics are troubling enough, the news media has contributed to a skewed public perception of minority youths: "News media unduly connects youth to crime and violence and [. . .] youth of color are overrepresented as perpetrators and underrepresented as victims of crime" (Dorfman & Schiraldi, 2001, 2). African-American youth, in particular, are overrepresented in media crime coverage compared to their actual rates of criminal activity; they are also underrepresented in reporting as victims of crime. In addition,

> youth of color fare far worse than their white counterparts in the media's association of youth and violence. A study of *Time* and *Newsweek* stories found that the term "young black males" became synonymous with the word "criminal" in coverage. A study on TV news showed that white youth were more likely to be featured in stories on health or education than black youth. (Dorfman & Schiraldi, 2001, 2)

The argument here is not that young people of color never make bad choices, or that their caregivers have no responsibility in providing a stable home. But when the statistics are as consistently lopsided as they are for school drop-out rates, foster care, and negative media representations, individual responsibility simply cannot be the only, or even the main, problem and solution. There is something else going on here, something I have referred to in this chapter as ideology. I use the term "marginalized" to refer to such youth to underscore the fact that something is being done *to* them by the institutions that are supposed to serve them. As we will see, the Writers' imaginative work regularly reflects their struggles to make sense of this damaging irony and to create alternative representations of their experiences and abilities.

CONCLUSION

Readers may feel that this chapter paints a bleak picture of the social realities of young people of color in the United States. My purpose is not to make readers feel sorry for The Writers, or to broadly condemn social service agencies, government policies, and the media—in fact, it is important to acknowledge that individuals working within these institutions often do so because of a genuine desire to improve people's lives, though such work is often hampered by the conflicting interests of the institutions as a whole. As is true for all of us, each of The Writers' lives is a combination of positive and negative experiences and influences. It is clear, however, that the writing of Patricia, TeTe, Marta, Robbie, Jig, Mekanismn, Crazy, Dave, and José grows out of their particular social situations, and is always at least partly a response to and/or a commentary on such situations.

As the rest of this book demonstrates, each of The Writers has the ability to be motivated, creative, and intellectually curious. My purpose in this chapter, therefore, has been not only to contextualize their lives and writing within public discourses on the intersections of race, ethnicity, poverty, language, and learning, but also to suggest some answers to two questions that are sure to occur to readers as they get to know The Writers: 1) How is it that youth such as these, with so much to say and such motivation to say it, remain largely bereft of cultural capital? and 2) Why do such youth so often, through their words and actions, demonstrate resistance to a society to which they could contribute so much? These are somewhat leading questions, and I take full responsibility for acknowledging at the outset of this book that I *do* believe that The Writers have much to say and much to offer. I hope that readers will come to similar conclusions, and will consider that the same is likely true of the youth in their own homes, communities, and schools.

3

"Questioning Myself and the People Around Me"

IDENTIFICATIONS AND COMMUNALITY IN IMAGINATIVE WRITING

Friday night open mike
Azteca Youth Arts Center, Chicago (from field notes)

While one guy is rapping, the others in the circle at the front of the room stand and listen, heads bobbing. If someone comes up with a really good flow, they smile and nod, or exchange a quick slide of fingertips, while the rapper continues his flow. There is an audience seated and responding, but within the circle everyone is a colleague, reacting as appreciative peers to skills they understand because they are honing them too.

———

Writing is a central way for The Writers to construct identity and claim membership in Discourses. For some acts of writing, the connections to a Discourse are obvious. The vignette that opens this chapter, for example, demonstrates the productive tension between individuality (the free-styling rapper who sets himself apart through specific verbal and stylistic flourishes) and community (the supportive peers literally surrounding that individual) always at play within social affinity groups (Gee, 1996) and the larger Discourses that inform them.

Identity play and experimentation with various Discourses are common markers of adolescent development, but as we saw in the last chapter, they are also political, particularly when the adolescents in question come from socioeconomically and ethnoracially marginalized backgrounds. The dialects, genres, and styles that a writer uses both reflect and challenge her social positioning, regardless of the content of a given piece of writing. Baugh writes that "speech can—and often does—serve as a social barrier *and* a (potential) badge of group identity" (1999, 137; emphasis added); the imaginative writing done by The Writers performs similar functions. Chapter Two focused on prevailing attitudes toward Black and Latino youths' words and actions; in this chapter, we will look more closely at the connections between the imaginative writing nine such youths create despite/in response to/independent of those attitudes, and the ways that their writing informs their intra- and interpersonal development. We will examine the ways that The Writers develop "identifications" (Baumann, 1999, 63) within affinity groups through their poetry, prose, and raps, and how those identifications connect to larger Discourses. We will also see how such identifications can at times empower young writers, giving them new or expanded access to individuals, institutions, and cultural capital, while at other times, the same identifications simply reinforce social and personal marginalization.

POETRY: AN INDIVIDUAL ART?

Poetry can *seem* purely individual, particularly given the romantic image of the solitary, tortured artist that exists in the popular imagination. Certainly, one often writes poetry by oneself, and writes about individual emotions and experiences. Yet while poets may write *by* themselves, they often write *about* their place among others, in conscious and unconscious ways. In addition, as Sheridan et al. (2000) point out,

> writing and reading are not social only through what is communicated, but also in the activity itself. Some writing and reading activities bring people together [. . .] while other writing and reading activities separate and isolate us from others [. . . but] these activities are all social in the sense that these literacy practices and their meanings have been constructed in cultural and historical contexts. (124)

Many of The Writers regularly share their work in one way or another; for some, it is this sharing that establishes them as writers to others and to themselves. Dave wrote for several years in notebooks and journals, but as soon as the paper in a book was used up, he threw it away. It wasn't until his cousin found one of these notebooks, "accidentally" (as Dave says wryly) read it, and told him that he should keep his work and should continue to write, that he began to do exactly that: "She told me to save them, and the way she talked to me, so passionately about saving them, I was like, 'Well, you know, why not?'" In fact, he says that after the conversation with his cousin, he tried to recover some of the notebooks he had gotten rid of. His sense of the quality and worth of his writing was powerfully influenced by this triangular interaction between himself, his cousin, and his written words.

Marta describes her poetry as both setting her apart from her siblings and establishing her identity in relation to them:

> I'm not that kind of person that tells my feelings; I keep them to myself mostly, so when I write poems it makes me feel better. So I usually write when I feel lonely, or I feel sad, or when I feel something's wrong with me.
>
> SW: Do you show them to people?
> M: My sisters, they sometimes read my poems. They like the way I express myself in my poems.
> SW: Do your sisters write?
> M: Sometimes my sisters write poems of their own, but most of all they like to talk about their problems, express themselves. I'm not like that.

In other words, Marta's sisters have established themselves as the ones in the family who talk about their feelings; Marta describes herself *in relation* to them as the one who writes instead.

José began writing poetry as a resident of Chicago's juvenile detention center; he has been a ward of the state since age 10, and his writing has often focused on family tensions. While the immediate motivation for José's writing might be viewed as personal, involving a particular family and its dysfunction, it is simultaneously a response to the larger social problems that foster dysfunction among poor, unschooled, ethnically and linguistically minoritized families in the United States:

> When I was in the Juvenile Detention Center, that's when I started writing. 'Cause I had a lot of time to think about the things I was doing, and to question myself why was I doing it, so after a while, I just started writing—questioning myself and the people around me: 'Is there any reason I'm doing it?' or, 'What's motivating me to do the things that I'm doing?' So I just started writing, and all of a sudden, a lot of things started falling into place, so I just kept writing.

Other pieces of José's early writing expressed his desire for a more secure social situation:

> Most of it was about me, how I wanted to be raised and how I was raised. Like, wishing that I was raised by a happy family without being abused. That's how I really wanted to grow up, but nobody gets to live how they want to live, so that's why I was writing like fantasy, everything that I wanted to be perfect I would write.

José started writing in an institution, and in the process of further institutionalization—on a bus heading toward prison—he recalls his need to write as so powerful that he thought he might go crazy if he could not:

> I recently got out of Cook County Jail, for some stupid stuff, for violating probation, and when I was in the cell for three days . . . I thought of so many stuff that it actually made me even cry, 'cause I couldn't get a pencil to write. All my emotions, if I don't bring it out, I keep it inside, and I get emotional, and I just need to write. If I don't write, I'm gonna have all these burdens inside of me, like what I did and what I didn't do.
>
>   I was in a cell in Maywood for three days with no phone calls or nothing like that. They moved me to Cook County jail for a week. And that week that you have in a jail doing nothing, trust me—you could write three books, if you really, really are dedicated you could. And that's when all my thinking started coming into place. Right when I got on the bus, I started thinking like, "Man, I wish my whole life was over," like . . . if I was [re-]born, I'd want to retrace all my steps that I did, and I didn't have a pencil so I started crying. I'm lucky I was in a cell, you know, 'cause I didn't want people thinking I, you know . . .

Interestingly, Dave's response to jail, as a writer, is the direct opposite of José's. With José's story in mind, I asked Dave if he, too, felt a strong urge to write when he was locked up. He said he did not, because

> I don't know if it makes sense—I was feeling trivialized. Ummm, like it didn't matter, what I wanted to be, or what I was, or who I am. It was like I'm just this number, that's all I am, nothing else matters. I don't know, maybe it's because I take everything in, like my family says, but that's all I could think about: "I'm nobody now."

Dave's response to institutionalization—that he has lost his selfhood, and thus his need/ability/desire for personal expression—seems the direct opposite of José's. In both cases, though, these young men were conscious of having a specific, writerly response to the situation. For José, the threat of social isolation brought on an intensified drive to communicate; for Dave, being numbered and compartmentalized rendered him mute. For both, changed social contexts engendered changed communicative stances—while the responses to these circumstances were specific to each individual, those responses were clearly also about the individual in relation to the social.

The connections that Dave and José make when they narrate their experiences of incarceration and writing are reminiscent of the relationships between writing and freedom, literacy and self-determination that have long been a marker of marginalized populations in text-centered societies. One of the most familiar representations of that relationship for Western readers is the slave narrative. While I don't mean to suggest that Dave's and José's situations are equivalent to those of slaves, there are similarities that are worth exploring in order to establish how ingrained the literacy/freedom trope is in U.S. culture. In Dave's and José's reminiscences on the one hand, and slave narratives on the other, freedom is literal. Their concern is first and foremost with physical freedom, geographical freedom—that is to say, the freedom to *move*, as well as the freedom to speak and act. In slave narratives, and in José's story—stories that start in captivity (in José's case, there is both the short-term captivity of incarceration but also the much longer-term "captivity" of being a state ward)—writing anticipates the literal freedom of movement precisely because speaking and acting can be mental as well as or instead of physical efforts. Writing of slaves' texts, Henry Louis Gates notes that they repeatedly suggest that "black objects could become subjects only through expression of the will to power as the will to write," indeed, that only through writing could one rise above "this relationship between the absence of selfhood and enslavement" (Davis and Gates, 1990, xxx).

Dave is an interesting counterpoint here, but his difference makes sense if we read his narrative as starting in freedom. Once in jail, the deprivation of freedom of movement creates in him a loss of desire to exercise the freedoms of speech and action. Since Dave was actually incarcerated for a brief time before he was bailed out, we can only wonder if his experience would have been part of a cyclical pattern whereby loss of physical freedom leads to loss of ability or desire to exercise the freedoms of speech and action, which losses in turn eventually lead to a building need to reestablish one's self, to write oneself out of captivity (both in the sense of using writing to argue for physical freedom and of creating a self-constructed identity through the telling of one's story). There is another way of reading Dave's experience, though, which is to recognize that while the literacy=social mobility "cultural model" (Gee, 1996, 78) is ubiquitous in U.S. society, there is a related cultural model that may remain less immediately familiar, though no less influential. While literacy is often a highly effective tool for socializing the poor into the status quo and their place in it, in many societies literacy has also been seen as "a possible threat if misused by the poor (for an analysis of their oppression and to make demands for power)" (Gee, 1996, 59). Thus, we see in U.S. history both compulsory schooling for the children of the poor and compulsory punishment for Whites who attempt to teach slaves to read and write; we see praise for Black authors at the same time that published work that challenges the status quo is often challenged in terms of authorship (in the case of, say, slave narratives) or of aesthetic quality and social responsibility (as in, for instance, rap lyrics). These conflicting cultural models play out at the societal but also the personal level, and can potentially either paralyze a writer or create overt and sub-textual themes that appear to directly contradict one another.

Here, then, is a situation that is relevant to one of the questions raised in the introduction to this book, the question of why The Writers' facility with certain kinds of writing has not resulted in great gains in cultural capital, as we are regularly told literacy does. The situation of American slavery caused slave narratives (whether recounted in books or abolitionist speeches) to effect change in the world, as, through publication and always with the support of White abolitionists, the voices of slaves were able to enter into the public sphere, to take part in the international conversation, to speak through writing with the authority of personal experience.[1] Slave narratives were written for a clear purpose and with a clear audience in mind—they were specifically and consciously created as social texts, and as such spoke to one another as well as to their readers (McBride, 2002). For the non-rappers among The Writers, this is the case, at most, in a very limited way. The four rappers, as this book demonstrates, do gain some cultural capital through their writing—they get respect from their peers and useful understandings about verbal communication through the process of writing in a consistent and focused way.

But there is another question that begs to be asked, and that is whether any of The Writers' work has the potential to move beyond affecting the individual to entering into public discourse in the way that slave narratives did so effectively. For six of The Writers, their texts could affect individual lives around them, but since none of them is pursuing widespread publication, they remain personal, at most local, in terms of audience. Even for the four rappers, who are writing for and in a very public Discourse, the possibilities of their texts effecting large-scale social change are small. Though they may talk about hip-hop in romantic ways, when it comes to their own involvement in it, the dream is not to effect social change, but to attain individual middle-class status. Social ills are the topic of many, many rap lyrics, but there are relatively few concentrated efforts on the part of artists or supporters to directly insert these texts, or the voices of the artists generally, into public debates in ways that might alter social realities. There are of course exceptions—early on, Afrika Bambaataa, one of the four DJ-fathers of hip-hop, saw the potential of hip-hop culture to redirect the energies and meet the needs of Black, urban youth and founded the Universal Zulu Nation. In 1989, KRS-ONE organized fellow rappers to record the song "Self-Destruction" after two murders hit close to home—a fan was killed at a concert, and KRS-ONE's Boogie Down Productions DJ, Scott La Rock, was a victim of gun violence. Though the song may have had some activating effect on those who heard it, it could not gain the mountains of attention garnered by, say, Quincy Jones's "We Are The World" project, given that rap was not yet the global commercial phenomenon that it was on its way to becoming. More recently, rapper Mos Def was arrested for staging an unsanctioned performance of his post-Hurricane Katrina song "Katrina Clap" outside the 2006 Grammy awards—yet the performance and arrest received little media coverage. Despite his sometimes socially critical lyrics, Kanye West entered the post-Katrina debate in a big way not through a song but by ad-libbing during a star-studded telethon, departing from the scripted plea for donations to state, "George Bush doesn't care about Black people." West's statement was not so much a positive activist move, though, as it was a protest *against* the lack of federal action in response to the blatant suffering of so many poor, Black people from the Gulf Coast.

What these examples suggest is that even for rappers who are explicitly attempting to influence public discourse through their words and performances, such attempts rarely result in widespread attention or action. How much more so, then, for people like TeTe, Mekanismn, Crazy, and Jig, who might occasionally address social ills in their lyrics, but who tend to state their long-term goals as rappers in terms of earning a living and gaining individual recognition rather than creating social change?

COLLABORATIONS WITH FAMILY AND FRIENDS

A number of The Writers specifically identify family members as primary influences on their writing. Robbie's father and brother are both visual

artists—his father, a painter who attended the School of the Art Institute
of Chicago, and his brother, a tattoo artist. He told me of a recent collaboration with his brother:

> Yesterday, I told him, "You know what, I'm gonna give you a
> poem, and you draw something, whatever you think it is," and he
> drew it. Then he gave me a drawing, and told me, "Write what-
> ever you think I think I drew." So I did; we did that yesterday,
> and it kinda came out pretty good.

Crazy, Jig, and TeTe have all grown up with a poet mother. When I
first got to know Crazy, he brought a book to school to show me; it was
an anthology of unknown writers around the country, and he wanted me
to see his mother's entry. Mostly, though, when I ask about influences,
both Crazy and TeTe talk about older brother Jig. They regularly go to
Jig for feedback and advice on individual raps and poems, so I asked
Crazy if this collaboration goes both ways:

SW: Do you critique your brother's writing too?
Crazy: Yeah. His stuff is always bad [*Bad* in this case meaning
         very, very good], you know? "How do you *do* it?", you
         know? I'd say out of the whole group, he's like, inside of
         8 Mile, he's like Rabbit [Eminem's character]. I'm like the
         Future [Rabbit's best friend]. Every once in awhile I can
         spit something cold like that, but it's like, him, he got the
         talent, and once you get that one opportunity, you gonna
         own everything you ever wanted. And I'm just the Future
         tagging along, you know, trying to push him forward,
         like, "Man, you can go for it, you can do it. As long as
         you know that you got your heart, you can do it . . ."
SW: Is he the best writer you know?
Crazy: Yeah (laughs). He is. Yeah he is.
SW: And the stuff he says to you when he's critiquing you, do
         you think he learned that somewhere?
Crazy: He taught his *own* self. Everything he knows, from com-
         puters, to painting, to writing, to whatever, he teaches his
         own self. He gets a little small helping hand, but from
         that, everything else he teaches himself.

Crazy's choice of comparison demonstrates a way that young people
use popular culture to frame their own experiences. He references two of
the main characters in the rap bildungsroman that is the film *8 Mile*. To

Crazy, Jig is B. Rabbit, the deeply talented battle rapper who is poised for greatness if he can only tame his inner demons. The character of Future is played by Mekhi Phifer and is based on Eminem's real-life best friend and long-time hype man, the rapper Proof (murdered in Detroit in 2006), who, like Future in the movie, hosted an ongoing freestyle battle event at a local Detroit club when he and Eminem were coming up. We assume that Future is himself talented—else how would he have secured his hosting gig?—but he recognizes Rabbit's skills as something special, something to be nurtured and supported. The movie thus provides Crazy with a language and reference that he can use to explain his own relationship to his brother and his estimation of his brother's talent.

Crazy, Jig, and TeTe all collaborate in various ways with friends as well as family, collaboration being as central as competition to rap. Marta is the one non-rap writer who tells of specific and ongoing collaborations with friends. In seventh and eighth grade, she and her friend Marisol regularly passed papers back and forth, composing what they titled "*Versos*"—brief rhymes in Spanish based on unattributable poems that, like urban myths and playground games, are omnipresent in youth culture. Marta gave me several pages of these; each four or five line *verso* is separated by a curved line split through the middle with a small heart. Marta's letters are clear, broad, and round, while Marisol seems to be trying her hand at the stylized script of her city's gang-affiliated taggers. The *versos* primarily deal with love and friendship; a few examples appear below:

Por ti suspiro
por ti me muero
y por ti en la escuela
me saque un cero. (Marta)
[For you I breathe
for you I die
and because of you, in school,
I got a zero.]

— —

En la puerta de mi casa
tengo una flor morada
como quieres que te olvide
si de ti estoy enamorada. (Marisol)
[By the door of my house
I have a purple flower.
How can you want me to have forgotten you
if I am in love with you?]

— —

Al primero eres hermosa,
A los 18 mucho más,
A los 20 eres esposa,
A los 22 eres mamá. (Marta)
[At first you are beautiful,
At 18 even more,
At 20 you are a wife,
At 22 you are a mother.]

Marta's individually authored poetry, like José's, is both personal and deeply connected to social relationships and experiences. She wrote her first poem in response to a friend's death at the request of the friend's mother; much of the prose writing she's done over the years has been in the form of letters written to a boyfriend, both before and after he went to prison. During the time that he was locked up, in fact, their relationship was purely, and powerfully, epistolary:

> I used to receive two letters from him every three days,
> and I used to write back . . .

SW: So you were writing a lot of letters for 5 or 6 months—

Marta: Yeah.

SW: Had he ever done a lot of writing before?

Marta: Before he got locked up, we used to write letters to each
other every day. I used to, when I was in school, I used
to write to him, and he used to write to me.

SW: How long would your letters be?

Marta: Two or three pages long.

SW: Why?

Marta: It was the same way, to express your feelings towards
each other. It was nice too, 'cause he used to put a lot of
nice things on the letters. I still have them all, all of
them. I have it locked up with a key, so no one could find
them and take them.

SW: There are kids that don't do a lot of writing, so the fact
that you were writing all the time—were you both writers anyway?

Marta: I feel like it was a way to express our love. We would just
write to each other. Like, we used to see each other too,
every day we used to see each other, and we used to
exchange our notes, and then the day after we wrote

> back. It used to be a habit that we used to have, all the
> time. After school I used to go to my house, take a
> shower and change, then go to his house and wait for
> him 'til he got back from work, and would receive the
> note, and he would jump in the shower, then he'd come
> out, I would have his supper ready, I used to cook for
> him, clean for him, and wash his clothes. We used to do
> everything together. We had a nice relationship. What
> messed it up was when he got locked up, that was the
> thing that messed up our relationship right there.
>
> *SW*:   This was when you were sixteen?
>
> *Marta*: Fifteen, sixteen.
>
> *SW*:   And then would you read the note while he was in the
> shower?
>
> *Marta*: [I'd] save them, save them until after we left, like the day
> after we'd read our letters and wrote back to each other.
> I used to love doing that all the time. I used to write to
> him during classes, and before I'd be writing to him,
> thinking about him . . .

Marta and her boyfriend used letters to bridge physical distance over which they had little or no control; Sheridan et al. (2000) argue that letters

> are one way that people contest current social and economic
> trends that pull friends, family and community apart. In this
> sense, community can be rebuilt through literacy practices. (270)

This is clearly the case for Marta, whose boyfriend's incarceration was, as we saw in Chapter Two, not only an individual circumstance but part of a deeply troubling social trend—that of the over-representation in prisons of males who are poor and of color. In general, we see that Marta is someone for whom writing, in various forms, is a central medium of communication. Her poetry, her letters—they are of a piece in terms of allowing her to express herself in a precise and permanent way to, or about, loved ones present and absent.

As we look in detail at how each of The Writers talks about his or her history and practices, then, we see that for each of them, writing means something different, and what matters about writing is distinct. For Crazy, for example, writing is connected to craft, to recognition, to a public Discourse he recognizes and wants to inhabit (or at least firmly believes that his older brother will enter). For Marta, writing is connected to intimate relationships, is in fact both a central element of and a response to such relationships.

EMPOWERMENT AND MARGINALIZATION

Some of The Writers express hopes for particularly tangible, concrete rewards from their craft. In the next chapter, the Maniacs talk about their professional plans and goals. Dave is the one non-rapper among The Writers who says that he hopes to turn his love of writing into a successful career. He is a prolific poet, an auto-didact who carries at all times a book and a dictionary, so he can look up the words he doesn't know. Recently, he read *The Autobiography of Malcolm X*; when he visited Chicago in early January 2004 (having recently moved with his mother to Miami), he and I spent an afternoon talking about the book, then sitting in his old room at his parents' house listening to recorded speeches by Malcolm X that Dave had downloaded from the Internet. He also updated me on his current project: inspired by the story of Malcolm X reading the dictionary front to back while in prison, Dave is now trying to read a page a day from the dictionary himself. I asked if he throws his new words into conversation, and he said that sometimes he'll practice them while he's watching his five-year-old nephew: "He'll say, 'Can we watch a movie?', and I'll say, 'Did you know that *abscond* means . . .?'"

For Dave, who started college in Miami in the spring of 2004, it seems at the moment unthinkable that he would commit the next several years to studying something not connected to his powerful creative impulse (his current plan is to study both creative writing and photography). But he recognizes that to do so will probably mean some sacrifice—in economic terms, certainly, but also perhaps in terms of the way others view him. For him, though, this is a source of pride, part of his ongoing project to become the kind of person he wants to be, as he explains to me in an e-mail about choosing between two potential jobs:

> I don't know how much of a difference pay is. The NIKE interview is Monday. But I'm setting my mind to never focus on money, at all. Even when I need it, I don't want to empower it by making it a factor in any decisions. I know most people will disagree with me. But how do other people in other countries live lives with their families and don't engage their mentalities in green? From birth, I'm told the importance of money. Why go to school? To go to college so I can make good money. The

```
dollar bill has plagued my thoughts since then. Now I'm
trying to rid myself of it.
```

Patricia sees writing playing a different role in her future. Despite the fact that "When [she] see[s] a plain piece of paper and a pen, it makes [her] want to write," Patricia, who writes poetry and some autobiographical prose, ultimately sees writing purely as an avocation. "Too much work, by the time you get out of school, too much school involved in that. But I want to do something involving my hands, and that's hair (laughs). But writing? I'll probably do writing in my spare time. Like besides anything else, I'll write." It has to be acknowledged that Dave may be in a better position to take the risk of making a go of professional writing—he has no children, and although he plans to help support his parents, there is less immediate financial pressure on him than on Patricia, who has two young children and another on the way.

José, a former *La Juventud* student who has yet to graduate from high school, has no stated plans to incorporate poetry into his paid work. His writing, though, reflects attitudes that might have an effect on his ability to successfully navigate official culture. His poem "Rebel Against Morals," part of which was quoted in the Introduction, reflects a clear oppositional stance:

> Who wrote these rules?
> Who formed these schools?
> Teaching us Lincoln freed the slaves,
> that Columbus discovered America.
> To learn about some great military leader,
> who killed off my ancestors,
> his face resides on the twenty dollar bill.
> Why learn all about this bullsh*t?
> Will it put money in my pocket?
> A roof above my head?
> Hell no
> F*cking hypocrites pumping the enemy into my brain.
> All of them are scared.
> Trying to put me to sleep,
> none of them will ever phase me,
> just create me
> to grow stronger
> to rebel longer
> and faster.
> *(Asterisks in original typed version)*

Accurate as José's critiques of U.S. educational ideology may be, being a rebel is not putting money in José's pocket or a roof over his head. José is trapped within a web of circumstances: he has no official status in the U.S. because his parents, who are residents, did not do the paperwork for him when they moved to the States. Because he has no status, he has no social security number. Because he has no social security number, he cannot find a job. In addition, the extreme instability of his family (which landed him in state custody by age 10) has left him with no real home. He occasionally stays with a relative, or with his girlfriend and her mother. DCFS (Chicago's Department of Children and Family Services) emancipated him at age 17; they usually help wards with transitional housing after they leave foster care (as they have for Patricia), but this didn't happen for José. So, while we can applaud his ability to recognize the ideological nature of the educational system and to attempt to resist his interpellation through it, this "critical consciousness" has limited influence on his concrete conditions (see Fine, 1991).

CONCLUSION

Complication and contradiction are inherent in much of the conversation and creative work of The Writers. Whether as attempts to understand their place in the world or to develop measures of which ways of writing and of being are worthy of respect, their imaginative work is both motivated by and reflective of the complexity that The Writers experience in their lives. Traditional academic writing, with its emphasis on developing clear arguments in order to prove a singular point, discourages if not complexity, then certainly contradiction. This structure, unfortunately, itself contradicts many young people's lived experiences, and may therefore alienate students from schoolwork that seems to require them to come to artificial, simplistic resolutions. Gee (1996, 102) observes that

> It is through attempts to deny this inevitable multiplicity and indeterminacy of interpretation that social institutions (like schools) and elite groups in a society often privilege their own version of meaning as if it were natural, inevitable, and incontestable.

Test questions have answers that are either right or wrong; essays require conclusions. It doesn't take much reflection to realize just how deeply and broadly this ideology of certainty infuses U.S. educational practice. If educators truly valued the critical thinking that is so ubiquitously referenced as a goal of schooling, then investigations that allow issues to retain their complexity would be the daily fodder of the classroom: "It is by stressing this multiplicity and indeterminacy—in the context of searching and on-going investigations of meaning—that the rest of us can resist such domination" (Gee, 1996, 102). Is it an accident, then, that the standardized tests and mandated curricula that characterize the current educational era leave little time for such investigations?

Educators working with young writers can intervene here by helping youth to conduct their own critical investigations in a focused way and to reflect that process in their writing—this is not to suggest that teenagers should only or all be writing polemics, but, rather, that the more aware writers are of the functions of ideology, the more they can interrogate and deepen the ideas that undergird their work. Adults are also well-placed to help young writers find ways to enter public sphere conversations, to make their accounts count beyond their immediate worlds. One has only to read a few of the poems and lyrics included in this book to see that The Writers have powerful stories to tell and critical perspectives on their social conditions. I would argue that it is the place of adults who want to see more equitable social conditions to help these youth find ways to become part of the story (Moje, 2000) in public and ongoing ways. This, of course, requires that such adults educate themselves about ways that this work is already being done—a subject treated in detail in Chapter Eight.

4

"You Gotta Be a Writer to Get in the Game"

UNDERSTANDING RAP AS A LITERATE DISCOURSE

"They shootin'—ah, made you look / You a slave to a page in my rhyme book."

Nas (Nasir Jones)
"Made You Look," God's Son (2003)

— —

"Every time I speak I want the truth to come out. Every time I speak, I want a shiver."

—Tupac Shakur[1]

— —

Rap is a complex Discourse. The central features of rap are counter to the social norm if the social norm is defined as the use of standardized English and compliance with a certain propriety in regard to public expressions of sexuality and use of public space. However, if we consider the marketplace as the ultimate arbiter of the socially acceptable, then rap can only be read as utterly normal, given its national and global popularity and the way that it has infused elements of society far from the playgrounds and housing projects of the Bronx where hip-hop first developed. Crazy, Jig, TeTe, Mekanismn—all of these writers are caught up in this complexity. They are continually developing their skills in order to earn ever-greater respect from an ever-widening audience of fellow participants in and/or fans of their chosen Discourse. Yet, ironically, while rap is performed primarily by the marginalized to gain or enact certain kinds of power, it simultaneously exacerbates social divisions by speaking in marginalized language forms about class-, race-, and gender-inflected topics.

1. THE BATTLE FOR RESPECT

For rap writers, empowerment takes many forms. The most widely visible is the money, fame, and "bling" that go along with the superstardom of a P. Diddy (aka Puff Daddy, neé Sean Combs) or a Jay-Z. In the neighborhoods, however, it's largely about respect and reputation. This is where battling comes in. Crazy explains:

> Battle rap? Is like somebody trying to come at you, like trying to shut down your name, usually they're starting something, trying to disrespect your name, make you feel like you ain't nothing, that you ain't got no talent . . . like street fighting, you know? You can talk all the talk you want to talk, but if you can't back it up then you ain't really nothing. But as long as you can back your stuff up, and keep your ground, then it's cool. If you win then you'll extend your ground and you're good.

Crazy tells the story of one battle that seems to have lost him a friend:

> Like the guy in my high school, he challenged me. I said "Don't steal my name"; he stole it. I told him "Don't answer back to my track,"[2] I'm gonna make him look [bad] at school, and, he answered back to one of my tracks, so I made a seven-minute, fifteen-second track and his whole name [was ruined] at the school. It means I shut him down, it's like he's nothing no more, 'cause he couldn't hold his ground. [SW: How did you win?] I played both of our tapes, and the school made me the champion. It was like, he ain't nothing but all talk, he say the same thing over and over again, just rephrasing. But me, I made seven minutes and fifteen seconds of everything different.[3] And I ate him up. . . . I didn't see him after that; I still haven't heard from him. [SW: In how long?] About a year (laughing). I don't know if he took it to the heart or not, I was just having fun.

While Crazy is confident about his ability to battle on tape, freestyle battling is a different story. In both cases, and not coincidentally, what battling resembles more than anything else is a contemporary version of The Dozens, the traditional African-American form of wordplay most widely known as the source of "yo' momma" jokes. Of course, it's one thing to exchange these barbs in the lunchroom or on the street corner; it's quite another in front of an audience that will respond with either appreciative shouts and applause or with boos and demands to get off the stage. Crazy again references the plot of the movie *8 Mile* when he admits that he shies away from such freestyle battles. "Why?" I ask.

> I'm scared. . . . Like at the open mike [described at the beginning of chapter 3], I froze and I couldn't do nothing. But I can't sweat over it, you know? It happened; it happens to the best of the people. But I just know that sooner or later, I'm gonna get my chance again, I'm gonna let it go, 'cause I'm gonna be better prepared for it . . . Like in freestyle it's easier, like if somebody's freestyling, I can do better to just listen to them and I'll be writing down every word I wanna do. But as far as coming out, too many things coming together, like I can't get the words out, can't put them together.

Rap has generated its own cautionary tale about taking battles too far. Mekanismn explains:

> The consumers, that's what they want—they want battling, they want the big artists to battle, [and then] they sell more records or whatever. But the long term, you know as long as it don't happen what happened before, you know, Tupac and Biggie. 'Cause now—[they're] just keeping it on wax[4] or whatever.
>
> SW: Do you think that could happen again?
>
> *Mekanismn:* I hope it don't, but you never know, you never know. It probably won't though. It'd be a terrible thing, for it to happen again . . . two rappers getting killed over different cultures. Over words. And it's really, you know, it goes deeper than the words, you know what I mean? 'Cause they didn't kill each other. So it's like, the consumers—people from outside. So, that's the big thing, the outside.

2. DEMONIZATION OF DIFFERENCE

As Mekanismn implies, each of the examples above works at different levels of audience. Battling is primarily internal—the freestylers and their judges participate in the same general Discourse, value the Discourse, and share an understanding of its norms. However, rap generally is a clearly and consciously public genre, arguably inviting the varied readings it gets from young fans, hip-hop heads (serious followers of the culture), parents, public officials, media representatives, and the general public. To some extent, the continuum between empowerment and marginalization through rap depends on who the audiences are and how much power their interpretations have in terms of practical consequences for either aspiring or professional rappers. Rap offers a clear example of what are, in many ways, incompatible perceptions; one can earn widespread respect and recognition for the same words and actions that can get one censured or worse. Robin Kelley describes one version of this dynamic within "gangsta" rap:

> Virtually all gangsta rappers write lyrics attacking law enforcement agencies, their denial of unfettered access to public space, and the media's complicity in equating black youth with criminals. Yet, the rappers' own stereotypes of the ghetto as 'war zone' and the black youth as 'criminal,' as well as their adolescent expressions of masculinity and sexuality, in turn structure and constrain their efforts to create a counternarrative of life in the inner city. (Kelley, 1994, 185)

The deeper one digs into representations of rap by the mainstream media and by the youth who listen to it and aspire to participate in it, the more one finds similarly incompatible perceptions. To take one example: Lisa Williamson, also known as Sister Souljah, came to mainstream attention during the riots that followed the Rodney King trial in 1992. This activist-turned-rapper "was publicly criticized by Democratic presidential candidate Bill Clinton for her ambiguous, aggressive comments regarding the 'logic' behind attacks on whites in Los Angeles" (Rose, 1994, 183). Because Williamson's recordings never garnered the widespread success of fellow political rappers Public Enemy, this is the only image that most non-rap fans would have of her. However, each time that I have run a book fair at *La Juventud*, at least one young woman asks if I have any books by Sister Souljah. These teens were less than 10 years old when

Williamson had her moment of public notoriety; what they know and respect her for are the books she has written since: a memoir (*No Disrespect* [1996]) and a novel (*The Coldest Winter Ever* [2000]) that speak to and about a specific kind of young urban Black female experience.

Writing in *The Atlantic Monthly*, Randall Kennedy charged Clinton with cynically using Sister Souljah as a way of

> assuaging fears that "progressive" politicians who attempt to be sensitive to the wrongs of racism will give away too much to racial minorities, particularly blacks . . . He wanted to show them [political conservatives] that he could stand up to blacks on their own turf and rebuff black guilt-tripping and mau-mauing. An array of black politicians and commentators assailed Clinton for "disrespecting" his host. But their highly public anger played right into Clinton's strategy: the more vociferous their denunciation, the more credibly Clinton could signal to white Reagan Democrats that he was courageously willing to offend his black allies, even if doing so cost him politically—though, of course, standing up to them was precisely the politic thing to do. (2001, online)

In a book about the Los Angeles rap scene that came out right around the time of the Rodney King verdict and its chaotic aftermath, Cross (1993) sums up rap's complex identity in relation to the dominant public sphere: "If rap itself as a word means anything it connotes 'talking'; this is its usage in African American slang. Ironically, however, within street language 'rap' also means 'a criminal charge', and as we head toward the end of the century the interchangeability of these terms has become *de rigueur* for the establishment" (64). Here again, as in the last chapter, we see verbal communication connected to freedom. Cross suggests that Black speech has become fundamentally criminalized. The First Amendment of the U.S. Constitution is supposed to protect against such a situation. Yet laws cannot fully adjudicate against social and cultural judgments. While a rap star *may* successfully defend him- or herself against attempts to censor lyrics in the courtroom, this doesn't mean that working class, Black or Latino teenagers freestyling on the corner or in the school hallway have any protection at all against the assumptions made by neighbors, local police, teachers, and school administrators about the teens' intelligence, educational and economic potential, or criminality. Such assumptions about marginalized teens' embodied texts have concrete consequences in all of these areas.

GETTIN' PAID

Writing is a notoriously unreliable career choice. Five of the writers in this study say that they *do* hope they might someday earn money from their craft, but it is significant that four of those five are rappers (the professional aspirations of the fifth, Dave, were discussed in Chapter Three). Rap is one of the few highly visible careers that provides young people with an attractive model for professional success in a writing-related field. Jig, Crazy, TeTe, and Mekanismn, along with several other friends, are part of a crew called the Maniacs. As the Maniacs, they plan to write, record, and distribute music, and to incorporate their various other abilities—Crazy's interest in graphic design, Jig's study of business and computer engineering—as they work together toward shared professional success.

These goals help to explain Mekanismn's consciousness of the importance of popular taste, which struck me when I recounted to him a conversation I had recently had with someone from Young Chicago Authors, a local program that offers free workshops to area youth and that sponsors an annual citywide poetry slam. I told him that the program's organizers aren't crazy about the slams because of the emphasis on competition—they said when you consider the teens who win the slam, it's not necessarily the best writers, but the performers who know how to "move the crowd" (in the words of the great rapper Rakim). Mekanismn praised such performers, saying, "That's marketable right there, what they did." He went on to explain how he fits his own activities to the marketplace: "I can freestyle; I don't really do it that much, though. But, as far as writing, that's my main thing, 'cause freestyle's not gonna get you paid, you know what I mean? You gotta be a writer in order to get in the game, and make albums, and make songs."

Just as Mekanismn expresses the commercial savvy one needs to be successful in professional rap, Jig's missives on the Maniacs' online site demonstrate a familiarity with the minutiae of running a business:

```
Subject: Business Update 12/26/03
Okay, we've got the files changin' and being listened
to, that's always good, but here's what's going on out-
side of the group.
We're close to getting our business license and getting
things rolling the right way, as well as making contact
with a couple more singers. Also, we are working on the
```

```
music for a couple of stores, one tentatively called "Ma
Sista Stuff" that will sell mostly lotions and soaps and
bath and body products from an exclusive distributor.
Then I also just got finished interviewing Nick Cannon
last week [Jig is a staff writer for his college's news-
paper]. Cool dude, but why is this business? Because in
the process I got in touch with some executives and man-
agers at Jive Records and BMG Records, and have gotten a
damn near shoe-in internship for either Jive or BMG.
Our Business Plan is almost complete, and we have gotten
access to a couple of studios now, and our own studio
will probably come around April, and negotiations with
Zoom Productions are in their final stages.
As most can tell, recording is going well, and so is the
writing. Look forward to some completely original work
to start being put in the next couple of months, and two
unofficial remixes in the near future.
```

Mekanismn's and Jig's words here combine to reflect a particular understanding of what it means to be a rapper in the twenty-first century. It requires a marriage of art and commerce—the most respected rappers are those who have become wealthy by branding their own images and then exploiting those images in a variety of commercial arenas while maintaining a reputation for superior skills on the mike. With his clothing line, record label, Manhattan club, and co-ownership of a pro basketball team (the New Jersey Nets), Jay-Z is arguably the ideal version of this type. The Maniacs are clearly committed to constantly developing their writing. Yet the rap Discourse in which they hope to become popular and (financially) successful prizes lyrical prowess as a necessary—but not sufficient—element for respect. There are Discourses within rap that value each of these two elements to varying degrees—the "conscious" or "backpacker" rap Discourse is primarily focused on lyrics, while a more recent Discourse has developed that claims to value financial success almost exclusively. Whatever the balance, the entrepreneurial and the artistic are both inherent to hip-hop, as becomes obvious as soon as we consider the first incarnation of hip-hop as DJ-driven block parties. There, the DJ was both artist and businessperson, creating the material conditions in which he (for it was usually a "he") could then perform while simultaneously earning money to further his craft and pay the bills, and so on ad infinitum.

THE GENERATION GAP

Now niggas can't make it to ballots to choose leadership
But we can make it to Jacob's[5] and to the dealership . . .
                                                    (West, 2004a)

Sitting atop a bench outside of *La Juventud* on a spring afternoon in 2003, the school's principal, an African-American man in his early thirties, tells me that hip-hop is a problem. He sees it as destructive, because of all the violent messages and bad language. As an example, he points out that on the best-selling rap CD of the moment, 50 Cents' *Get Rich or Die Tryin'*, the rapper poses on the cover aiming a gun toward the viewer.[6]

I had been telling him about the breakdancing competition I had seen the previous Friday night, and how there seems to be this really cool basis of respect running through all of the hip-hop elements (breakdancing, rapping, turn-tabling or scratching, and graffiti). He didn't see this as the case; to a lot of the positive things I brought up, he said that it *used to* be that way, but not now: "Now it's all gangsta or bling-bling." He says he has these debates all the time with friends in their late 20s. He also says that he can assure me that someone like Mekanismn would not listen to that kind of stuff. I told him that, in fact, Mekanismn had just told me that he *did*, that he likes both hip-hop (a term sometimes used to define the deeper, more introspective and/or socially conscious style of rap) and rap (the term sometimes used specifically for the ubiquitous money-diamonds-sex-violence style). I added that Mekanismn had said that his own CD, which is "more-or-less ready" to put out locally, is mostly rap.

— —

In 1996, Lisa Sullivan identified a widespread Black generation gap and the public attribution of that gap, in magazines like *Time* and *Newsweek*, to "gangsta rap and hip-hop culture." However, Sullivan argues that "the eclipse of Black civil society has much more to do with the institutional collapse of the inner city and the failure of traditional Black social and civic organizations to mobilize, organize and empower the most isolated and abandoned among the urban poor" (1996, online). Blaming hip-hop is easy, especially when critics can point to convenient, if largely circumstantial, evidence of the negative effects of rap music on Black youth. Linguist and self-appointed cultural commentator John McWhorter does exactly this when he reports on a scene in a restaurant during lunchtime, where several young Black men who appeared to be skipping school were causing a scene with their loud behavior:

What struck me most, though, was how fully the boys' music—hard-edged rap, preaching bone-deep dislike of authority—provided them with a continuing soundtrack to their antisocial behavior. So completely was rap ingrained in their consciousness that every so often, one or another of them would break into cocky, expletive-laden rap lyrics, accompanied by the angular, bellicose gestures typical of rap performance . . .

Many writers and thinkers see a kind of informed political engagement, even a revolutionary potential, in rap and hip-hop. They couldn't be more wrong. By reinforcing the stereotypes that long hindered blacks, and by teaching young blacks that a thuggish adversarial stance is the properly "authentic" response to a presumptively racist society, rap retards black success. (2003, online)

As the analysis in Chaper Three demonstrates, McWhorter's claim that rap can have negative social effects is not wrong, just incomplete. There is certainly much in rap to be offended by; there is also much of value, both artistically and politically. Certainly, the outright dismissal of an entire genre, and by extension of the generations that developed it and grew up in it, seems misguided. Instead of dismissing the genre because of its more notorious elements, adults—black, white, red, yellow, whatever—might attend more closely to the meanings that young people make of the various elements of hip-hop, and to the extent to which they are a continuation of older cultural elements rather than a severing of old values and standards. Near the end of an essay on hip-hop that Mekanismn wrote for a high school class, he articulates the meaning hip-hop carries for him:

That's what hip hop does; it brings people together. It's almost like a blessing from God. I know it is for the street cats because it gives them the extra strength to keep going and make more hip hop music. Black people got to love this something that they made, because what they were subjected to and had to go through brought this hip hop, a beautiful movement that everyone could appreciate.

For Mekanismn, hip-hop provides evidence of resourcefulness in the face of oppression, of historical continuity, and of hope. Educators and others who aim to work effectively with youth might consider hip-hop an invaluable site for listening in on a conversation that opens out on a

multiplicity of issues central to kids' lives. With just a small bit of familiarity with the genre (which can be easily and productively gained from
students themselves), teachers can bring the generational, racial, gendered, and economic issues surrounding and infusing rap into the classroom in order "to focus students' attention on relevant aspects of cultural
models, in the students' home culture, in their multiple other social identities, and in mainstream and school culture" (Gee, 1996, 89). Thus does
mutual learning occur—teachers help students develop critical analyses of
the texts surrounding them, while students bring the teacher to a fuller
understanding of *how* rap means to its primary audience.

ROLE MODELING

As we have already seen, the primary Discourse within which several of
The Writers develop and perform identities is hip-hop. That Discourse
encompasses everyone from the kid in his room listening to the new Jay-
Z CD to Jay-Z himself. One has only to watch a young, local emcee to
recognize the influence of existing hip-hop norms—in terms of clothing,
performance style, language, and so on—on his or her identity construction. This influence has been the topic of much debate and criticism, particularly because of the emphasis in some sub-genres of rap on drinking,
drugs, casual sex, and material accumulation.

Of early hip-hop, record producer Bobby Robinson said, "It's kids—
to a great extent mixed-up and confused—reaching out to express themselves" (Toop, 2000, 85–86). This is what's often forgotten in debates
about the responsibility of rap artists to set positive examples for young
listeners. The fact is, many of the biggest artists in rap were, until very
recently, the same kids that the public now says they should be role
models for. Talib Kweli and Mos Def, two artists commonly held up as
positive, critical, socially engaged rappers, have pointed this out, noting
that it is unreasonable—or at least unrealistic—to expect that a rapper
like 50 Cent, for example, having come from a background of drugs and
violence, is going to magically transform into an upstanding social model
because he's become a recording star.[7] Kweli further suggests that there
is, in fact, a powerful positive message to be read in 50 Cent's career—a
message of literal and figurative survival (not only was 50 famously shot
nine times, but his mother, a drug addict, was shot to death when he was
a child). This is a generous, but I would argue also a necessary, interpretation. Kweli is one of the more respected rap lyricists in the game. Not
coincidentally, he, Common, and Kanye West (two other rappers
respected for their social awareness) are all sons of college English profes-

sors—in fact, West's mother Donda has written a memoir about raising her son (West, 2007), and she, Kweli's mother Brenda Greene, and Common's mother Mahalia Hines, along with Mos Def's mother Sheron Smith, a nurse, are part of what Greene calls "an informal network of hip-hop mothers" (Greene, 2007, 20). By publicly refusing to criticize a rapper like 50 Cent, Kweli and Mos Def implicitly acknowledge that he is a product of his primary social context, as they are products of theirs. They can no more claim fully individual responsibility for their socially critical stances than 50 should bear completely individual responsibility for his focus on gaining as much fame and money as possible (which even "conscious" rappers will admit they are not actively trying to avoid). To do so would be to willfully ignore the place of social positioning and cultural capital as influences on an individual's ideological perspectives.

The rap fans among The Writers are, of course, engaging with rap texts through their own social positioning and familial ideologies; thus, they consciously and unconsciously choose among a given artist's explicit and implicit messages for those that fit the morals and values they have already internalized. This critical factor in engaging popular culture is not uncommon: "[P]eople often choose content that agrees with their own values and interpret conflicting content so as to support these values" (Gans, 1999, 44). The other messages they take not as guidelines for how to live but as expressions of solidarity and of common experience. Dyson argues that Tupac Shakur communicated these often-conflicting messages more powerfully than most:

> Tupac was not hip-hop's most gifted emcee by any of the criteria that define the form's artistic apotheosis . . . Above all, Tupac was a transcendent force of creative fury who relentlessly articulated a generation's defining moods—its confusion and pain, its nobility and courage, its loves and hates, its hopelessness and self-destruction. He was the zeitgeist in sagging jeans. (2001, 106–107)

Another popular rapper under regular attack during the research phase of this study is Eminem. This artist is something of an anomaly—a White rapper who has achieved incredible popular success while earning and maintaining respect from critics and fellow artists. He is also a rapper whom the writers in this study seem able to read in complex ways. There's no denying that many of his songs either directly highlight or else imply violence, misogyny, homophobia, and drug use. These are clearly problematic topics, particularly when the audience for them includes children. Yet many have pointed out the sometimes fantastical, comic-book exaggeration of Eminem's presentation of these subjects. Writing about *The Slim Shady LP*, Robert Christgau said, "Anybody who believes kids are naïve enough to take this record literally is right to fear them, because that's the kind of adult teenagers hate" (qtd. in Bozza, 2003). In addition, Eminem is at times a gifted reflector of shared experiences, as in the song "Lose Yourself" (2002), which rappers of all stripes have cited as an accurate representation of the underground rap battling experience:

> He's nervous, but on the surface he looks calm and ready
> To drop bombs, but he keeps on forgetting
> What he wrote down . . .

For all the uproar over Eminem's allegedly misogynistic, homophobic, violent lyrics, the fact is that songs like "Lose Yourself" tell kids like Crazy, TeTe, Jig, and Mekanismn that it's okay to be scared, that success takes time, that failure is a lesson, and that talent alone is not enough. Is Eminem a role model? He has adamantly refused the label, mocking, in his song "My Name Is," the very notion that anyone would want to emulate someone who has led such a messy life:

> Hi kids, do you like violence?
> Want to see me stick nine-inch nails through each one of my
>   eyelids?
> Wanna copy me and do exactly like I did?
> Try 'cid and get fucked up worse than my life is?

What his songs tell kids over and over again is that his childhood sucked but he's okay, that he had to struggle before he made it, that things aren't always great even after you achieve success. For the rap writers in this study, empowerment comes not solely from getting respect for good lyrics; it also comes from the realization that others understand and have lived through the same experiences, and that one can gain some measure of control over those experiences through writing and public performance.

AGENCY AND IDEOLOGY

> It seems we living the American dream
> But the people highest up got the lowest self-esteem
> The prettiest people do the ugliest things
> For the road to riches and diamond rings
> We shine because they hate us, floss 'cause they degrade us[8]

> We trying to buy back our forty acres[9]
> And for that paper, look how low we'll stoop
> Even if you in a Benz, you still a nigga in a coop.
> (West, K., 2004b)

Conflicting messages are generated not just in terms of the language that marginalized young people use, but in terms of what they're supposed to believe. They understand that history has contributed to their positions near the bottom of the socioeconomic ladder. They understand that any social changes that have occurred have been the result of communal struggle, as with the marches, arrests, and violence of the civil rights movement. This understanding of the absolute necessity of social support for individual and mass success is evident in some rap lyrics. For example, Tupac Shakur's early song "Brenda's Got a Baby" (1991) begins by pointing out the futility of seeing individual life circumstances as unconnected to the larger community. After Tupac begins the song by announcing that a young, unschooled local girl has given birth, a voice in the background says, "That's not our problem, that's up to Brenda's family," to which Tupac responds, "Well let me show you how it affects the whole community."

Nas's song "Dance" is an ode to his mother, who died during the making of his album *God's Son* (2002), and whom he honors as "the strongest person he ever met" and as a woman who "raised a family in the ghetto," acknowledging in the process the pretense of claims that one has truly made it on one's own. Yet young people also hear, and readily internalize, messages reinforcing the American myth of social mobility through sheer individual effort. "You can do anything you put your mind to, man," Eminem says at the end of his song "Lose Yourself" (2002). "I know I can be what I want to be / If I work hard at it I'll be where I want to be," a group of children chant in Nas's "I Can" (2002).

These conflicting ideologies are evident in Michelle Fine's book *Framing Dropouts* (1991), in which she investigates possible reasons why students drop out of school. What she found is that many who drop out do so at least partially because they recognize that schooling is ideological, that its purpose is to assimilate students into a culture that, because of their own experiences and observations, they either resent or see as making promises it won't fulfill (in terms of education automatically equaling social mobility). This is similar to the findings of ethnographer Paul Willis (1977), who studied a group of working class males in England, and found that they, too, had partial insight into the ideological nature of formal education. In both cases, however, the partiality of the insights tended to stop short of any active, political response. Instead, both Fine and Willis argue, youths' resistance to the ideologies the schools emphasize simply causes them to withdraw. Ironically, this resistant response to the dominant ideology ends up reinforcing it, in the sense that such youth end up reproducing the social structure by remaining in a low economic position because of a lack of education—a crucial, although not in itself sufficient, bestower of cultural capital. Critiques of higher education can be equally double-edged. Statistics show that "earning a bachelor's degree raises median annual income by 75 percent over a high school graduate—from \$33,373 to \$64,474" (Advisory, 2001, 4). This makes it critical that the conversations about schooling that show up in popular media aimed at youth are picked up and continued in homes, classrooms, and community centers.

It is not a bad thing that the Afrocentric group dead prez (2000) say the following to their listeners in a spoken passage at the end of the song "They Schools":

> They ain't teaching us nothing but how to be slaves and hard workers for white people to build up they shit / that's why niggas be dropping out that shit . . .

While dead prez is the kind of overtly political rap group that tends to attract older and more politically engaged—also, ironically, probably more formally educated—listeners, one of the biggest releases of 2004 offered similar sentiments to a much broader audience. *College Dropout*, a CD by Chicago producer-turned-rapper Kanye West, features a motif of the uselessness of higher education that runs throughout many of the songs and skits on the record. The second single off the CD, "All Falls Down," criticizes young people who matriculate for no purpose other than to meet outside expectations:

> Man I promise, she's so self-conscious
> She has no idea what she's doing in college

Later in the CD, we hear one of several spoken pieces, this one called "School Spirit Skit 1":

> So now you get your degree tattooed on your back you're so excited about it. If you continue to work at the Gap, after several interviews, oh my god! You'll come in at an entry-level position and when you do that, if you kiss enough ass, you'll move up to the next level, which is being a secretary's secretary! And boy is that great, you get to take messages for the secretary, who never went to college. She's actually the boss's niece, so now you're a part of the family . . .

There is obviously more than a pinch of reality in West's ironic take on the touted benefits of higher education. The question is, where does this leave the teenager who may sense that there are limited prospects for someone entering the work force with only a high school diploma—to say nothing of not having a diploma at all?

The common thread in many of the critiques of schooling included here is the idea that such challenges are not welcome within school walls. This is a place where adults can usefully intervene, to contribute to "the creation of space where teachers and students can engage each other in an educational discourse beyond that of the dominant ideology" (Sheridan et al., 2000, 263). Admitting to young people the reality that education does not always deliver on its promises, that there are biases inherent in much of what passes for "history," "literature," and so on, and that formal education reflects the same contradictions that exist across social institutions, is a significant step in helping students develop sophisticated critical skills—skills one cannot develop in a context where questions and challenges to the status quo are unwelcome.

IDENTITY PLAY

> Do I contradict myself?
> Very well then I contradict myself,
> (I am large, I contain multitudes.)
> —Walt Whitman, "Song of Myself"

Sick Wicked (of The Maniacs)—08:55pm Jul 19, 2003 EST

```
Ayo, this is my remix to X-tina's "Dirrty," well at
least the rap part, hope ya'll like it.
Artist: Christina Aguilera f/ Sick Wicked (of The
Maniacs)
Song: Dirty (Unofficial Remix)
Album: Untitled
Sick Wicked's Verse:
I wake up at night
Right around 3:30
Tear this muthafucker down
If the party ain't dirty
Chickens surround me
Probably 30
Had to dismiss a few
Cause they stink from herpes
```

Dudes smell like ammonia
Girls smell like fish
Digging my fork inside of my favorite dish . . .

Jig (of The Maniacs)—11:04pm Jul 19, 2003 EST

damn Sick, you takin the boards over, i'm feeling that,
you got a weird ass sense of humor dawg fa'real

7/19/03 Instant Message conversation between author and Jig

sueweinst says:
Hey, I'm just reading your latest posts. Can I ask a
quick question?
Jig says:
yeah, wassup
sueweinst says:
Ummm . . . didn't you tell me that Sick Wicked is
your alter ego?
Jig says:
lol yes
sueweinst says:
So you're basically talking to yourself
Jig says:
lol that's about the size of it lol
sueweinst says:
Very funny. I'm enjoying it.
Jig says:
don't tell no one that Jig and Sick Wicked is the
same person though
Jig says:
i'm just having a little fun, seeing who is going to
catch onto it
sueweinst says:
No, I would never.

— —

Identity construction has always been central to popular culture. The
most successful and well-known architects, like pop icon Madonna, have
acknowledged this and played with self-representation in ways that garner
reactions ranging from respect to outrage, depending to some extent on
how clearly the beholder understands the process of conscious manipula-

tion of self and audience that is occurring. Those who are less able to maintain a critical distance from their own self-construction, like Tupac Shakur and Kurt Cobain, have often become overwhelmed by the weight of their images.

An unwillingness to pin down meanings is evident throughout hip-hop. Producer/rapper Dr. Dre, discussing the meaning of the title to his hit "Nothing But a G-thang," says, "G-thang, ghetto-thang, gangster-thang, whatever you want to make it" (2003). Tupac Shakur famously reclaimed the word *thug*, developing a philosophy of "THUG LIFE" in which the two words became an acronym for *The Hate You Give Little Infants Fucks Everybody*. For him, individuals who embodied this philosophy were those who came from nothing, and perhaps continued to have nothing, but who nonetheless made lives for themselves with a sense of pride and Discursively defined ethics. The word *pimp*[10] has been used throughout hip-hop culture in both literal and figurative ways—sometimes *pimp* literally refers to someone who makes money by selling the sexual labor of others (see the discussion of rapper 50 Cent's song "P.I.M.P." in Chapter Five), and sometimes it refers to someone who is in control of his/her life and business, handling both with style. Rapper Nelly was criticized by several African-American organizations for naming his energy drink "Pimp Juice." Yet, in the song of the same name that inspired the drink's title, Nelly defines his terms in this way: "Now your pimp juice is anything [that will] attract the opposite sex / It could be money, fame, or straight intellect" (Haynes et al., 2002). He further indicates that pimp juice transcends gender, race, and class—you, reader, might have pimp juice and not even know it! It is hard not to see these examples of young Black men flipping the script on negative mainstream connotations of words as mirroring their attempts to similarly challenge mainstream views of their demographic—as we see The Writers doing throughout this book, rappers regularly insist on their right to define their own terms, to take control of their own representations, and to challenge negative social perceptions with and through writing and performance.

Similarly, there is in rap an insistence on claiming multiple identities, multiple personas: Is Marshall Mathers Eminem or Slim Shady? Is B—, one of the writers in this book, Jig or Sick Wicked? TeTe is a nondrinking, nonsmoking, 16-year-old virgin who writes lyrics like:

How many places? There's just too many places
Like doin it in the bedroom and riding niggas' faces
I be that bitch that's handlin the shyt
Not afraid of it
I'm runnin this shit . . .

TeTe refers to herself in the third person while talking about the distance between herself and her rap alter ego (TeTe is her rap name, not her given name):

> Tete, she's like the total opposite of me, I don't usu-
> ally shout or . . . but Tete, she's loud and ghetto and
> proud of whatever she is [laughs]. She's loud. And
> she gets anybody's attention, and she said what she
> said, and you won't understand, or you just won't be
> able to look.

SW (to Jig):   How do you feel about your 16–year-old sister talk-
               ing like this?

Jig: To me, it's like, it's rap, it's a freestyle, you know.
               But *I* say some crazy stuff.

TeTe: Right. 'Cause he won't do half the crazy stuff he say.
               And I won't do ninety percent . . . Like what you
               can hear on my raps, I do say, "I'm a virgin, and I
               won't do this." When I rap, I correct it at the end,
               "I'm a virgin . . ."

SW: Are there other artists who influenced you to write
               the TeTe kind of stuff?

TeTe: Like Eve, and actually, Trina actually, I listen to her,
               'cause Trina, if you listen to her on the interviews,
               she'll sit there on the interview and be quiet, calm,
               and when she raps she'll do all this stuff, like Sick
               Wicked type of stuff.

Jig: Yeah, a lot of people they see Trina totally different
               than what she is.

TeTe: Yeah, you listen to her in the interview, she'll be a
               lady.

Jig: She went through almost four, five years of college
               and everything. Only reason she left college is
               'cause she got the record deal. And she had a B, like
               a B+ average. She's not dumb at all [laughs].

TeTe: Yeah, she was like a cheerleader, and . . . You could-
               n't *pay* me to do most of that [laughs]. Like she a
               totally different person. And, Eminem, like the stuff
               he say on records, you'll be like, 'No, he's crazy,' but
               you'll see him with his baby, and he's, like, with the
               little girl in his movie . . .[11]

Jig: Yeah, he'll be like, people come up and talk to him,
               he's like one of the nicest people, and he had one of
               [his daughter's] friends sleep over, and [when the

	friend got sick] he called the parents and everything to find out what to do, take her to the doctor and everything.
TeTe:	And he loves his daughter. But you wouldn't think that by the stuff . . .
SW:	'Cause he does talk about his daughter, right?
Jig:	That's one thing, a lot of stuff, he can play around a lot, but if somebody end up mentioning his daughter, he'll be like, starts getting off the wall [laughs]. Next time you heard Eminem talk about Ja Rule, it was like, 'Oh my god.'
SW:	So Ja Rule said something about . . .
TeTe:	Yeah, he said like, "Kim is a alcoholic/you're momma's a known slut/ [Jig joins in for the last line] so I wonder what Hailie's gonna be when she grow up." And you don't *say* that . . .
Jig:	Right. That's like the third time somebody said something about his daughter, and each time, he retaliates, he gets like, ugly. He becomes a different person.
TeTe:	He becomes . . . Slim Shady [laughs].

Even when a young rapper sticks with one rap identity, the option to change names in order to remain distinct always exists. I realized this when talking to Mekanismn, whom I had remembered as having a different "tag":

SW:	Wasn't it Q-Mecca?
Mekanismn:	Yeah, it was Q-Mecca, then I upgraded a little bit . . . Everybody had the name Mecca, so I wanted something different than everybody else. So, actually, I started recording my songs on Maxell tapes, and it had [the word] *mechanism* on there, in the regular spelling [. . .] So I'm like 'Yeah, that's my name,' and all this, and then I got my spelling, M-E-K-A-N-I-S-M-N. It's different, you know?

If the modern era was characterized by a desire to resolve contradictions through the establishment of core truths, then the postmodern era is characterized by hip-hop's refusal of easy solutions, clarifying explanations, or calls to mainstream versions of social responsibility—all while the genre generates billions of dollars in profits for its biggest artists, producers, and record companies.

KEEPING IT REAL

There is an interesting distinction between identity play and *fronting*—pretending to be what one is not—in hip-hop. As we saw in the last section, taking on different identities is a common and accepted practice among young writers. Yet at the same time, "keeping it real" is a basic requirement for respect among rap artists and fans. Careers have been destroyed over revelations of inauthenticity—for people aware of pop culture in the late 1980s, two words sum up this pitfall: "Vanilla Ice."

More recently, popular rapper Ja Rule was caught telling stories about himself that weren't true, causing some fans to dismiss him. Steve, one of the regular contributors to the Alicia Keys freestyle message board, wrote a rhyme about his disdain for Ja Rule. When asked about it on the boards, he said, "That fool pissed me off trying to be too much like Pac [Tupac]." The conversation continued:

.:::*Ms Felony*:::.—03:47am Jul 9, 2003 EST
```
Hahaha.
I wonder why everyone sees that resemblance. I mean,
hell yeah, that shit's obvious, but what makes you think
that he's emulatin' Pac's style?
I need a convo, Steve. LoL
```

Steve- 04:02am Jul 9, 2003 EST
```
LoL Okay
#1 He's always trying to wear that damn bandana like Pac
was (lol)
#2 He keeps sayin that he's the next coming of Pac
#3 He trys to act like he was some hardcore gangster
when everybody else knows and says that he never ever
was like that
#4 He said so himself, he once said he wants to be just
like Pac.
```

Even for those who are not viewed as pretending to be what they're not, who are seen as keeping it real, we have to recognize that there is a certain amount of image packaging that occurs with any highly successful public person. The question is, to what extent is what sounds like autobiographical writing mediated—by the tastes of the marketplace, the requirements of record labels, the need to develop a "rep," and—for young local writers like those in this study—the desire to construct oneself according to forms already established by popular rappers (e.g., writing about being a thug, not because one has necessarily thought of oneself that way in the past, but because that's what Tupac called it, and then incorporating into one's lyrics not only the term itself, but the "identity kit" that goes along with that term). It is fair, productive, and educative for socially committed adults to ask such questions of young people in ways that are respectful of youths' own identifications and cultural commitments.

LITERARY COMMUNITY

Rap always has been here in history. They say when God talked to the prophets, he was rappin' to them. You could go and pick up the old Shirley Ellis records, "The Name Game," "The Clapping Song," Moms Mabley, Pigmeat Markham, when he made "Here Comes the Judge." You could pick up Barry White with his love type of rap, or Isaac Hayes. You could get your poetry rap from Nikki Giovanni, Sonya Sanchez, the Last Poets, the Watts Prophets. You could get your militancy message rap coming from Malcolm X, Minister Louis Farrakhan, Muhammad Ali. A lot of time, the Black people used to play this game called The Dozens on each other, rappin' about your mama or your father, and stuff. And you could go back to the talks of Murray the K, Cousin Brucie, and all the other radio stations that was pushing the rap on the air or pushing the rock and roll. So rap was always here.
        —Afrika Bambaataa (in Frick & Ahearn, 2002, 76)

— —

There is a form of community that I have not touched on yet. It both leads to and grows out of the writing of marginalized peoples; it spans both time and space; it positions the young writers of today within a long, if severely under-recognized, historical tradition. The fact is, Black people have been representing themselves and their experiences through oral and written texts for centuries:

The act of testifying or giving testimony has deep roots in African American history, reaching back to slavery (and before), to the places our ancestors created—behind somebody's wood cabin doubling as a makeshift church or meetinghouse, or in a nearby clearing—where they opened themselves up to one another, showed their scars, spoke of their day-to-day life, their hopes and dreams, prayed to their God, and tried to remember everything they had lost. (Tarpley, 1995, 2)

Some of these moments of self-representation are included in standard school curricula: students may well read excerpts from a slave narrative and the lyrics to some of the old slave songs; they will surely be introduced to a few of the most celebrated authors of the Harlem Renaissance; and they will almost certainly read sections of the oratorical masterpieces of a Frederick Douglass or Martin Luther King Jr. Alongside these canonical works, however, exists a wealth of unknown writers and texts.

The Black pulp fiction of the 1940s through the '70s has gone the way of much pulp fiction: it has a cult audience, but as far as mainstream culture goes, it may as well not even exist. Yet, for many rappers, particularly those who fall into the "gangsta rap" category, this genre is a central influence, often acknowledged overtly within lyrics and through visual homages. One of the most popular influences of this kind is Chicago writer Robert Beck, aka Iceberg Slim, and his autobiography, *Pimp: The Story of My Life*. Rappers like Ice T and Ice Cube pay homage to Beck through their chosen names. Leila Steinberg, a friend and mentor of the late Tupac Shakur, still has Shakur's book collection. Along with diverse titles ranging from literature and philosophy to feminism and conservative social commentary ("Pac paid for this to attack it," Steinberg says of E.D. Hirsch's *Dictionary of Cultural Literacy: What Every American Needs to Know*), the collection features "the riveting corpus of Donald Goines, the Detroit writer who specialized in brutal tales of black street life and who died prematurely and violently" (Dyson, 2001, 95–96). Goines' *Black Girl Lost* (2001 [1973]) became the basis for—and title of—a song on rapper Nas's 1996 CD, *It Was Written*.

Another subgenre of rap, sometimes labeled "conscious rap," often categorized as part of or connected to the Native Tongues school (an early '90s movement that included De La Soul, A Tribe Called Quest, and Queen Latifah), draws from a different line of literary forebears. New York's Last Poets and Los Angeles's Watts Prophets were two groups of Afrocentric spoken word artists who emerged in the late 1960s and early 1970s. Anyone who was shocked by the angry political rhetoric of late '80s rap group Public Enemy was clearly not paying attention about 20 years previously, when these spoken word performers communicated Black Panther-style ideologies through strikingly straightforward, angry texts. Their recordings are still available, and their words have been sampled and/or referenced on cuts by "socially conscious" artists like Common and Nas, as well as "gangsta" rappers like N.W.A. (Niggas With Attitudes), although, in the latter case, not always in ways that reflect the Poets' original message. In a conversation between Last Poet Abiodun Oyewole and former N.W.A. rapper Ice Cube, Oyewole refers to N.W.A.'s referencing of the Poets' piece, "Die Nigger":

Ice Cube:	Now, what we have today is some rappers want to put knowledge in their records, and some rappers don't. You got the older generation of so-called leaders want to come talk to us, want to sit down and rap to us. But it's no dialogue there. They always let the small things or small differences interfere with the bigger picture. If I use the word "bitch," to me it's just language.
Abiodun Oyewole:	But language does control. Language sets us up for a whole bunch of things. Language incites us. That's why when we used words like "bitch" in the Last Poets, we made it clear that those words were not used loosely, but *specifically* to talk about a particular character in the community, not everybody. It really hurt me when N.W.A. sampled us on "Real Niggers Don't Die," and they sampled "Die Nigger," and they had, I think it was, "Niggers die, niggers die for 400 years. Die, nigger, die, nigger, die, nigger, die." But *then* the brother comes in and says, "Real niggers don't die." And they missed the most important part, because the poem says, "Niggers watch Nat Turner die, niggers watch Emmett Till die, niggers watch Medgar Evers die, watch niggers die, die, die. Die, nigger, die, nigger, die; they can die so black folks can take over." And that's the point, get rid of the nigger, you get rid of the bitch, so that the beauty of your folks will emerge.
Ice Cube:	But I can't go to the Japanese talking Chinese. I have to speak the language of the street to get their ear. See, the teacher, the preacher, the politician won't talk real to the kids. So that's why they won't listen to them. You got to talk in their language and guide them to the place, and that's exactly what we're doing . . . (Rule, 1994, 171–172)

Despite the unresolved disagreement in this conversation, the fact that Ice Cube and Oyewole are engaging in a dialogue makes this a far different situation from the intergenerational conflicts we saw in Chapter Three. Instead of dismissing one another's ideas and forms, there is, here, an attempt to communicate and to understand. This kind of public conversation is exactly the stuff of which quality work is made. The value of recognizing one's place within an ongoing artistic tradition is that one has standards to measure oneself against, has elders to work with, play off of, rebel against. One is, in short, accountable—in order to effectively enter this ongoing conversation, one must understand the conversation, and one's work must in some way respond to the conversation. So by encouraging young people to engage with the forebears of the current art forms they value, we ultimately encourage attention to history, to literary movements, to political struggles . . . we encourage, in other words, a high standard of intellectual and artistic engagement.

Of course, in order to encourage such engagement, we must first examine our own biases in terms of what counts as literary, as intellectual. McWhorter (2003) tells us that rap, Last Poets–style spoken word poetry, the speeches of Malcolm X, the political treatises of the Black Panthers, and so on, are an aberration without deep historical or cultural roots:

> The venom that suffuses rap had little place in black popular culture—indeed, in black attitudes—before the 1960s. The hip-hop ethos can trace its genealogy to the emergence in that decade of a black ideology that equated black strength and authentic black identity with a militantly adversarial stance toward American society. (Online)

The idea that angry rhetoric regarding the African-American experience suddenly appeared in the 1960s is, to put it kindly, inaccurate (see, for example, David Walker's infamous *Appeal*, an 1829 pamphlet that exhorted slaves to rise up against their oppressors: "It is no more harm for you to kill a man who is trying to kill you, than it is for you to take a drink of water when thirsty"). McWhorter seems to take it upon himself to identify what is or is not part of black popular culture. For him, the writing of Iceberg Slim, Donald Goines, and Chester Himes clearly is not, but neither—if we take anger and an "adversarial stance" as the measure—are James Baldwin or Frederick Douglass, among others.

(SUB) CULTURAL LITERACY

To what extent are rapping activities connected to specific subcultures? And does it matter? Well, it might, especially given arguments about standardized curricula that stem from calls for "cultural literacy," in which culture is seen as singular and unified. The argument, verbalized in E.D. Hirsch's popular book of the same name, is that members of a society must have a core of common references, must understand themselves as participating in a shared history. The problem is that to speak of the United States as comprising a single, unified culture is to act purposely blind to the messy, multiple, sometimes conflicting reality of how a society of such mass develops. If culture is "that level at which social groups develop distinct patterns of life, and give *expressive form* to their social and material life-experience" (Hall & Jefferson, 1976, 10), then it takes nothing more than a walk down a busy urban street to recognize that there are many subcultures active within the überculture that we call "American." How are we to understand the connections and disconnections between so-called subcultures and that which we call American? Hall and Jefferson offer an approach:

> Groups which exist within the same society and share some of the same material and historical conditions no doubt also understand, and to a certain extent share each others' 'culture.' But just as different groups and classes are unequally ranked in relation to one another, in terms of their productive relations, wealth and power, so *cultures* are differently ranked, and stand in opposition to one another, in relations of domination and subordination, along the scale of 'cultural power'. The definitions of the world, the 'maps of meaning' which express the life situation of those groups which hold the monopoly of power in society, command the greatest weight and influence, secrete the greatest legitimacy. The world tends to be classified out and ordered in terms and through structures which most directly express the power, the position, the *hegemony*, of the powerful interests in that society. (11)

The fact is that young people participate in various subcultures, which simultaneously develop out of their "social and material life experiences" and reimagine or reconstruct such conditions. Among The Writers, the rappers are most clearly identifiable as participating in a specific literate subculture, and their engagement with literacy seems strongest when they are able to use it to "express [their] life situations." It is in their texts that we find evidence of the very connections Hirsch calls for, either directly—through references to Tupac and Biggie, say, or Malcolm and Martin—or indirectly, through the use of styles that have a history within the subculture. These references help them to make connections and forge understandings; the extent to which they feel unable to work from such references, styles, and histories in the classroom may well be the extent to which they grow increasingly disengaged.

It is perhaps inevitable that the creative, socially engaged and engaging acts of young, marginalized writers will elicit complicated and sometimes incompatible perceptions, as such youth have been raised on intensely complicated narratives of creative action. It is through these narratives that many of The Writers are able to both develop and express certain understandings about social and interpersonal relations in ways that most adults would find positive. Two recent examples of these models are Tupac Shakur and Biggie Smalls (aka The Notorious B.I.G., nee Christopher Wallace). Each of these men was a popular rap artist in the early 1990s—Biggie in New York, Tupac on the East Coast and then in L.A. Tupac's mythology was already well under construction during his career—son of a single mother who was an ex-Black Panther-turned-crack-addict; named for an Incan hero who defied the Spaniards; raised to think one man his father only to find out, as a teenager, that another man actually was; student at a high school for the performing arts in Baltimore who drifted into petty criminality as his mother plunged more deeply into addiction; a stint in prison in New York; the move out west to become a member of the Death Row record label . . . The press played up an east coast–west coast feud, primarily between Sean "P. Diddy" Combs' Bad Boy label in New York (for whom Biggie recorded) and Suge Knight's Los Angeles–based Death Row (Tupac's label), a feud that Tupac was all too willing to jump into. And then Tupac was shot dead in Las Vegas, while driving in a car with Suge Knight. A year later, Biggie was shot dead on a visit to L.A.

The longer-standing mythologized pairing, for African-American youth and others, is that of Martin and Malcolm. These two gifted, murdered leaders have been set up as more dichotomy than dialectic. There's the pacifist and the insurgent, "we shall not be moved" versus "by any means necessary." Black hat, white hat; good guy, bad guy—death has a way of stripping the influential of their humanity and re-creating them as culturally useful archetypes. Clearly, neither man in life was so easy to pin down—Martin Luther King was passionate and powerful; Malcolm X's enacting of actual physical violence ended before his career as the "radical" leader ever began. King visited Chicago and realized that an absence of legal segregation was not equal to an absence of segregation; at the end of his life, he was shifting from "race talk" to "class talk," developing a poor people's movement when he was shot dead in Memphis. Malcolm X ultimately came up against the limitations of the Nation of Islam's race-based philosophy, returning from his Hajj to

Mecca more committed to Islam and therefore less convinced that race is always the end of the conversation.

The dichotomy of Martin and Malcolm, and the limits of dichotomization, play out in hip-hop as in other cultural Discourses. Spike Lee ends his most powerful film, *Do the Right Thing*, with the "by any means necessary" quotation from Malcolm X on the screen. In an interview about Shakur, the actress Jada Pinkett Smith, a close friend of the rapper from their days as students at the Baltimore School of the Arts, explains their different paths by saying that she was raised on Martin, while he was raised on the Black Panthers and Malcolm X.

Artists across the rap spectrum have invoked Martin and Malcolm at one time or another, and it is through hip-hop that we can see the limitations of the dichotomized view—both for rappers and listeners, and for the genre's and the young fans' critics. But hip-hop also demonstrates the ways that, despite a continuing allegiance to the Martin/Malcolm split, Black youth enact their racial and ideological identifications in rich and complex ways.

CONCLUSION

Rap lyrics, like other popular art forms, often explicitly or implicitly challenge dominant social values, "mock[ing] the attitudes and pretenses of those who have power over us" (Newkirk, 2002, 77). Finally, any act of writing is political in that it represents a speaking subject, however infused that subject is with received ideologies. Rap, prose, and poetry can allow the historically silenced to speak, and it is this that often renders such practices threatening to those who have been traditionally the sole occupiers of public discursive space. For those who are invested in broadening that space, however, youths' imaginative writing—their "accounts"—provides a site of possibility. If we want to see their accounts count for some larger public, the first step is to make clear to the young people we work with that these accounts count to us.

5

Pregnancy, Pimps & "Clichéd Love Things"

WRITING THROUGH GENDER AND SEXUALITY[1]

In previous chapters, we have examined the ways that imaginative writing produces and reflects particular identifications for The Writers in terms of social class, race/ethnicity, dialect, and communities of practice. In similarly rich and complex ways, The Writers engage with themes of gender and sexuality in and through their work. Looking at their poems, lyrics, and prose, it is possible to see these young adults negotiating gendered roles and trying out various ways of "doing" sexuality. Even the fact that these young men and women choose to write can be discussed in terms of gender stereotypes of communication and literacy. This chapter will begin with a brief examination of such stereotypes before moving into an examination of the rich, varied, and complex ways that The Writers construct and revise gendered selves and sexual personae through their written texts.

A note: For the purposes of this chapter, I define *gender* as the range of socially constructed norms for performing masculinity and femininity, and *sexuality* as the physical/erotic identities one performs in action and language. These are distinct but related categories, and this chapter moves back and forth between them in ways that I hope make both the distinctions and the relationships clear. It is also important to note that all of The Writers self-identify—to me and, as far as I have seen, to the public generally—as heterosexual, and their writing reflects that identification.

LITERACY AS GENDERED PRACTICE

Assumptions abound about the connections—and disconnections—between gender, communication, and literacy. Females talk; males act. Young women embrace, or are at least comfortable with, reading and writing; young men resist. Women are from Venus; men are from Mars.

The realities are both more complicated and more interesting. Among The Writers, as should be clear by now, we have both males and females who embrace writing in a variety of genres and for a variety of purposes. Their composing practices and products at times appear to reflect traditional gender roles and at times complicate or confound them. One example: despite widely held assumptions about male lack of interest in verbal and written communication, I found it much easier to identify male writers for this study than female. Yet this very fact may simultaneously reinforce certain beliefs about the social functions of gender, that is, that males have traditionally been the primary actors in public spheres, and females in private. According to such notions, my greater difficulty in identifying female writers means not that females are less interested or active in imaginative composition, but that they simply do it less publicly, share it less openly. Following this brief analysis, I would have to conclude that the male writers in my study are exceptional in their writing practices but representative in their comfort with public performance, while the female writers are typically feminine in not making a public spectacle of themselves.

Such an analysis would afford us little, however. While individuals do perform gendered identities, gender itself is not monolithic—the qualities and parameters of particular gender constructions shift with shifting contexts. Nonetheless, a number of studies support the male-resistance-to-literacy thesis. Newkirk (2002) claims that young men view literacy as feminine, and so resist reading and writing: "Girls . . . can construct workable identities that include positive attitudes toward schoolwork and literacy. For boys, and particularly African American boys, the role tension is far more extreme" (40).

Paul Willis (1977) puts the feminization of literacy by boys into a British class perspective. Writing about working-class "lads" in a factory town in England, he demonstrates the complex ways that working-class masculinity leads these young men to reject the "theoretical"—of which essayist literacies are seen to be part—for the practical. The factory men's experiences transmit to the young men of the community the shop-floor wisdom that "an ounce of keenness is worth a whole library of certificates" (56). Willis argues convincingly that in an economy in which working-class boys are likely to follow their fathers into the factories, the lads "reverse the valuation of the mental/manual gradient by which they are measured" (148). Since masculinity is so highly valued among the lads, "manual labor is associated with the social superiority of masculinity, and mental labour with the social inferiority of femininity" (148). Willis points out that while this association is useful to the lads in that it instills manual labor with cultural and social capital, it unfortunately relies on the continuation of a rigid sexism: "If the currency of femininity were revalued then that of mental work would have to be too" (149).

Yet Willis's study is not a simple reinforcement of the standard boys-don't-write stereotype. In fact, his work serves as a powerful caution against making causal arguments about individuals' practices based on a single characteristic such as gender. For Willis's lads, concrete experiences of class, culture, gender, and schooling interacted to generate a resistance to reading and writing. For the male poets and rappers in the present study, different versions of these same variables have generated a passion for certain kinds of writing. This does not mean that there is no point in attending to gender in examinations of literacy practices, but that attending to it in isolation does not produce useful understandings.

Smith and Wilhelm (2002) summarize the research on literacy and masculinity as saying "that boys will go to great lengths to establish themselves as 'not female' and follow what their peer group establishes as gender-specific behavior. If reading or other literate activities are perceived as feminized, then boys will go to great lengths to avoid them" (13). That "if" is significant—in a group of friends in which imaginative writing is viewed positively, the danger of feminization for male writers is not an issue, though this is not to say that others outside of the friendship circle will share that view. Interestingly, Smith and Wilhelm conclude that literacy in general is neither feminized nor rejected by the young men in their study:

> One reason the battle lines are misdrawn is because there are boys and girls on both sides. Though people often must necessarily think in generalizations and categories, these are always too simple, and . . . the cost of oversimplification is too high when it comes to boys and literacy. (Smith and Wilhelm, 2002, 9)

What *is* resisted by many of their subjects is school literacy, and the authors conclude that it is resisted not because it's "girl stuff," but because it is "insufficiently social" (among other things) compared to the out-of-school reading and writing that the young men tend to do, or to share, with others (147).

Meanwhile, research on girls and literacy also complicates standard assumptions. Daphne Key (1998) presents the stories of six African-American women who once saw themselves as writers, but who received social messages that inhibited—or completely ended—their engagement with imaginative writing. Key suggests that despite commonly held stereotypes of literacy as feminine, girls and women may resist public acts of literacy out of fear of "being perceived as 'incorrect'—and having one's incorrectness confirmed by possible spelling, usage, reading, or speech errors" (5). Cushman found that surface performances by young people can't tell us everything we want to know about their practices. Among the seven- to nineteen-year-olds in her study, "no one . . . wanted to be seen as standing distinct from their peers" (59). Thus, youths often avoid appearing *too* smart, *too* literate, *too* . . . anything. But in Cushman's study, as in the present one, appearances belie reality: "Many female teens found ways to obviate these group dynamics. They hid books and writing tablets around their house" and individually requested that Cushman supply them with books by Black women writers (59–60). Like rubbing a pencil on a sheet of blank paper pressed against an engraving, in private and among intimates, publicly invisible literacy practices often emerge.

POETRY: FOR GIRLS ONLY?

In my years of teaching English, I have been confronted a number of times with the concept that writing—and poetry in particular—is "for girls." TeTe tells of a male friend who saw poetry writing as emasculating:

> *TeTe*: He wouldn't write poetry . . .
> *Stella (TeTe's friend)*: He thinks that makes you gay or something.
> *Jig*: Sometimes when people think of poetry, they usually think of love, stuff like that. Poetry can be anything. 'Cause I write about anything.
> *Stella*: Jig doesn't do stuff like that. He says, "Roses are *dead* [all laugh], violets are gray."

In this exchange, TeTe and Stella start out sounding dismissive of their friend's ideas about poetry. Yet both Jig and Stella go on to imply that it is acceptable for males to write poetry primarily because poetry doesn't have to be about "love, stuff like that"—in other words, about presumably feminine—or "gay"—topics.

For some males, the one acceptable reason to write poetry generally and love poetry specifically is to attract females who will, hopefully, see it as a romantic and sensitive gesture. These young men also think that poetry is "for girls," but in a way that actually motivates them to write. Dave remembers this as the reason he started writing in sixth grade:

> It was one of those grammar school girlfriend/boyfriend things. Of course, I was trying to be different from most of the other people, so I tried to write stuff. But it was mostly really clichéd love things. And then I would read it; like the girl would like it, but I'd be like, "This sucks." So I tried to write other things, and I started to write a little bit more.

Robbie has a similar story, about one of the first poems he ever wrote:

> [A friend] told me to write this poem, for this girl he liked . . . I wrote this poem, and he got the girl. And this girl was like, *she* writes poems; she was like the head of the poetry club in his school, and she could swear it was like the best poem written by someone, and . . . right now they're gonna get married after high school, and that's my poem, you know? I still hear her recite some of the words.
>
> *SW*: Does she know you wrote it?
> *Robbie*: She kind of got an idea after about a year, 'cause she would be at the house and so would I, and we were kind of all friends, and she kind of knew that I was the artistic one . . . So she kind of got the idea, but she was still like, whatever, the thought of him giving it to her anyways was the best.

Although these young men say that they began composing poetry for girls, they have developed into prolific, committed writers. Significantly, despite their early poems, both Dave and Robbie are now careful to distance themselves from what Stella and Jig define above as feminizing subject matter. Dave now dismisses the "clichéd love things" that populated his early pieces, and Robbie expresses surprise that the girl in question liked his poem so much because "that's like a love poem, and I don't *do* love poems." Among both male and female poets in this study, then, certain kinds of poetry remain clearly gendered, and the young male who writes unironically, or without ulterior motives, about love risks being marked as feminine/homosexual by even those of his peers who embrace a writerly identity.

YOUNG WOMEN DEFYING STEREOTYPES

> Gentlemen, ladies. If you please—these
> are my wicked poems from when,
> the girl grief decade [. . .]
> My first felony—I took up with poetry . . .
> —Cisneros, 1992

Sandra Cisneros calls her poems wicked, and calls the taking up of poetry a felony. Her words suggest that to express oneself fully, to act as though one's experiences and emotions matter in the world—to engage, in short, in so self-centered an act as writing, is to verge from the role of a proper female. Gilligan and Brown (1992) reinforce this perception, suggesting that for young women, communicating their own ideas and experiences can feel like pretty risky business:

> Girls at the edge of adolescence face a central relational crisis: to speak what they know through experience of themselves and of relationships creates political problems—disagreement with authorities, disrupting relationships—while not to speak leaves a residue of psychological problems: false relationships and confusion as to what they feel and think. (214)

For Patricia and Marta—both of whom have already crossed over the "edge of adolescence"—imaginative writing has provided an outlet for such speaking. Patricia's work addresses difficult personal and social issues head-on—excerpts of her autobiographical narratives about growing up in public housing and about the experience of pregnancy appear further on in this chapter. Marta's poems, as we have seen in previous chapters, speak to her own and others' experiences of death, incarceration, friendship, betrayal, and love. For these two writers, poetry and prose help to make sense of their experiences as well as to occasionally communicate those experiences to others.

There is another function that imaginative writing performs for young women. While composition is always to some extent an act of identity construction, there are certain situations in which that purpose for writing appears particularly conscious. In a study of middle school girls at a special school for "youthful offenders," Margaret Finders reports that the girls "engaged freely in literate activities . . . They used reading and writing to prove they were bad, and they proved it through their bodies. They spoke, read, and wrote about their sexuality" (2002, 94). Finders suggests that these writers are constructing a consciously essentialized identity in response to their external social positioning. Similarly, TeTe follows the model of a number of popular female rappers in composing an aggressive sexual persona through her lyrics. She says that this kind of persona is necessary if she is going to hold her own among her brothers and the other male members of the Maniacs; her identity work through composition therefore seems driven by both generic norms and personal aims. Marta and Patricia write, instead, about love, about loss, and about family and life experiences. For all of these writers, though, their composing practices allow them to take some measure of control over their own representation. This is a particularly powerful act for individuals from communities so consistently represented by others, and for others' purposes, in the public sphere.

RAP AND GENDER

As mentioned above, Margaret Finders found that students at a school for juvenile offenders seemed to have a great deal invested in the identity of "badness" that had caused their exile to the special school in the first place. However, "badness [at the school] was distinctly gendered. Males . . . displayed their prowess through their criminal offenses. Girls, on the other hand, displayed their prowess through their sexuality" (2002, 89). Tricia Rose (1994) finds a similar phenomenon when she examines the lyrics of popular rappers:

> Like their male counterparts, [female rappers] are predominantly resistant voices that at times voice ideas that are in sync with elements of dominant discourses. Where they differ from male rappers, however, is in their thematic focus. Although male rappers' social criticism often contests police harassment and other means by which black men are "policed," black women rappers' central contestation is in the arena of sexual politics. (146–147)

In both cases, males' thematic focus is in the realm of public behavior, while females' focus is in the traditionally private sphere of sexuality. Anyone with a car radio knows that male rappers also spend plenty of time addressing sexuality. Yet the sources above suggest that in Discourses that emphasize "badness," the options for claiming badness are more circumscribed for young women than for young men. Male rappers do talk about sex, but they also talk about police brutality, about criminality, about the experience of being a young, Black man in the contemporary United States. In the current rap climate, female artists primarily

focus on one issue: sex. This is not to say that their work is not inflected
with issues of race, class, etc., but that for females other elements are
often subsumed under the principal category of sexuality (see Bettie,
2002). To put it differently, both males and females experience race and
class in gendered ways, but the algebra of this social triad varies:

> The rise of female MCs in the late twentieth century represents
> an ongoing musical saga of black women's issues concerning
> male-female relationships, female sexuality, and black women's
> representations from a working-class point of view (Keyes, 2004,
> 188)

In other words, while there is a strong tradition of raw sexuality expressed
in women rappers' lyrics and performance, it is a race- and class-inflected
sexuality. Even when female rappers are not overtly addressing race, their
words situate them: "Using words uncommon in mainstream romantic
pop or jazz songs, women of the blues affectionately refer to their male
lovers as 'Papa' or 'Daddy,' while women of rap refer to their male com-
petitors or lovers as 'sophisticated thugs' or 'niggas'" (Keyes, 2004, 187).
In her song "Single Black Female" (Jones et al., 2000), the rapper Lil' Kim
explains the work that sexuality does for the female rapper, while using
terminology that does indeed situate her in the ways described above: "If I
talk freaky—then that's my business / If I dress freaky—then that's my
business." This lyric communicates two messages quite clearly—talking
and dressing "freaky," or in a frank sexual manner, is her business in that it
is her *decision*, and it is she who will deal with the repercussions of that
decision. Clearly, though, "freakiness" is also her business in that it's her
work, her way of establishing and maintaining an artistic reputation and
career. Such self-consciousness is a direct response to the criticism that
women who exploit their own sexuality for profit are simply—or only—
dupes of a masculinist ideology. Certainly, there are still useful debates to
be had about the ultimate productivity of a raunch-as-empowerment philosophy, but to categorically condemn such a tactic is arguably as patriar-
chal a move as making it the only way for women to gain voice.

TeTe's overtly sexual lyrics are in line with the styles of popular
female rappers like Lil' Kim and Trina. Again, the significance of discursive norms is clear for not only her, but the male Maniacs as well. Jig,
Crazy, and Mekanismn all occasionally write about personal experiences
and warm emotions. Yet they also produce what, for me, is a surprising
amount of violence- and/or sex-filled lyrics, given that I have come to

think of all three as particularly respectful and thoughtful young men. Is this their way of establishing, if not an identity of "badness," then one of "manhood"? Given its history, it is understandable that rap is a central site of masculine gender construction. Toop notes that

> since rapping has strong roots in the predominantly male activities of toasts and dozens, it is not surprising that men see it as the musical equivalent of a sport like baseball. They are prepared to accept that women can do it but see the competitive element as the final deterrent . . . Women associated with the scene, on the other hand, feel that men tend to disapprove of their standing in front of a crowd bragging and boasting. But in some cases they go along with the men: shouting about yourself might be all right when you're young but as you get older it's 'unladylike.' (2000, 94–95)

The influence of popular female rappers' poses on her own thematic choices seems clear from the signature line TeTe uses in her posts to the Keys message board. It is a lyric from Da Brat, a female Chicago rapper: "Shit fuck y'all niggas, you can't live without pussy/Be disrespectful and get no more nookie . . ." This aggressive stance has everything to do with control, and for Da Brat and TeTe, sex is the site where females can exercise control over men most powerfully, in this case through the age-old threat of withheld "nookie." TeTe says that her sexually explicit lyrics started out as a way to get her older brothers' attention as a writer:

> It's like, when you grow up . . . and everybody else is already doing something, I want to come out and let everybody look at me like, "Man, I'm gonna notice *her* . . ." I've always been the youngest [in the family], and I'm the only girl [in The Maniacs] . . . So, if I put something out, I want them to be like, "*Man*, hold on, let me stop and retrace."

The strategy seems to have worked, as TeTe has become a full member of the Maniacs. I couldn't help but ask her brothers if their younger sister's explicit lyrics made them uncomfortable. Not at all, they said. Apparently, such subject matter and language is so established an element of the female rapper persona that TeTe's brothers are able to separate what they clearly see as writing-to-generic-norms from their sister's everyday personality.

GENDER AND SEXUALITY AS CONTENT

Love, sex, masculinity, and femininity are central themes in adolescent writing. Young people internalize the stereotypes and contradictions that pervade society; their writings often reflect hegemonic assumptions with striking clarity. In the following rap, Crazy reinscribes a classic sexist trope, that of the good girl/bad girl, madonna/whore—or as he puts it, the sista/bitch:

> Jay Z said it best
> I love my sistas
> But I don't love no bitch . . .
> To gain a female
> With the strength of a sista
> No matter the ethnicity
> Cause a sista keeps her soul
> A bitch takes a toll
> A sista keep your feet
> A bitch splash the grease
> A sista bring you heaven
> A bitch leaves at 11
> That's why I love my sistas
> But I don't love no bitch.

While one might be tempted to make judgments about Crazy's general attitudes toward women based on the preceding lyric, the following poem confounds easy judgments. This time, Crazy not only does *not* essential-ize women through familiar stereotypes; he takes the unusual step of writing a poem from a woman's perspective:

> I once chose you to be my defender
> and the man who would uplift my spirits
> with the tenderest touch one lady can find.
> I sensed that you would be there and not
> destroy me. I see now that I was wrong.
> You showed me a beautiful picture, but the
> meaning behind it left nothing but pain.
> So wonderful to the outer world but inside
> is what I leave. A picture that has yet
> to come together and be complete.

Dave demonstrates a similar contradiction. His poem "Bitch" (which he dedicates "to those scandalous females") expresses exactly those sentiments that we see in Crazy's rap above:

> Why we treat you bad you can't understand
> push play and hear Eminem's Superman[2]
> you got a pussy and know how to use it
> lookin' good, can't no man refuse it
> your actions leave us in mad confusement
> you a bitch
> don't be surprised at the naming
> otherwise you a ho in training
> not all women
> are part of this web I'm spinnin'
> only those who play stupid games
> gold diggin hoes
> searching for the nigga with the nicest Rolls
> can't make shyt for themselves
> gotta have a man to have shyt
> bitches who think they can fuck with our minds
> spit at us some sexy ass lines
> and for them we'll wine and dine
> but we ain't all that foolish
> some of us seen past the lies
> behind the truth that ya'll denies
> so stop being a leech with a pussy and breasts
> I will be laid to rest
> before I fall for you
> and write conned on my chest
> become a real woman
> and hold your own
> get yourself a home
> make yourself rich
> and then I'll stop calling you bitch

Despite this strong expression of resentment—even anger—toward women, Dave too can move beyond stereotypical, misogynistic postures to show his affection for and vulnerability with women. In "A Female Deserves Better," he laments his inability to give his woman what she wants and needs, but hopes she'll love him anyway:

It don't matter how much you try
for her you live or for her you'll die
remember the day might come
where you'll do wrong and she'll run
with a question mark written across your face
you'll ask why
it's 'cause a female always deserves better
she should always have more than she has
more lovin', more respect, more honesty
my girl gives life to that which rots in me
and I treat her well
but when we argue I can't help but yell
and I don't help her out as much as I should
now I realize that she always deserves better
'cause she's given more to me than I lent her
ain't no man measure up to a female
can't step into her footprints or walk her trail
when my temper rises up and my forehead angrily burns
she'll wait for my patience to return
deal with my bullshyt and troubles
but she still deserves better
better than I can give her today
but I'll try to persuade her to stay
'cause I know that she deserves more than me
but I hope it's me she wants.

The tensions among both Dave's and Crazy's writings about women make clear that gender and sexuality are no less complicated for young men than for young women; for everyone, personal experiences combine with received wisdom from family and friends and with popular images and representations to create conflicting ideas about who and what men and women are and how they relate to one another. Rap, one of the powerful purveyors of social types for young people, including both Dave and Crazy, provides no clear answers. Many of the most popular male rappers suggest that a real man is one who controls women, who gets what he wants from them without falling victim to their gold-digging or possessive ulterior motives. At the same time, there is an almost-as-ubiquitous theme in rap (and in Black culture historically) of paying homage to the ultimate woman: "Never disrespect a woman 'cause I love my mama," Talib Kweli raps in "Know That" (1999); "Even as a crack fiend, mama/you always was a Black queen, mama," Tupac rhymes in "Dear Mama" (1995), one of the songs most closely identified with the late rapper.[3] There are also songs that present complicated images of the lives of young women in urban America. In "Heaven Only Knows," artist and actor Eve raps honestly about her previous life as a stripper while filling in the context behind the image:

> Thought it was cute to flirt with older cats up in they face
> Didn't have a daddy so I put a daddy in his place . . .

Dave and Crazy both have mothers and sisters, both have had girl friends and girlfriends, both watch movies and music videos and listen to rap and other musical genres. All of these influences are brought to bear on their developmental struggle to make sense of male/female relationships, sexual and otherwise. Their apparently contradictory poems, reflecting both distance and empathy, are no more contradictory than their own experiences and the representations they see all around them.

The young women in this study also use imaginative writing to address gender-specific issues, although in different ways—or, perhaps, for what seem like different purposes. Patricia and Marta both write poems that deal with relationships. Marta's poem "My Boyfriend's Prayer" expresses both love and anxiety:

> Dear Lord,
>> Full of grace
>> Bless my boyfriend's cutie face,
>> Bless his hair that always curl'z,
>> keep him safe from other girls,
>> Bless his eyes so green & nice
>> make them see the morning light,
>> Bless his arms so big & strong
>> make them stay where they belong,
> Heavenly father from above
> please protect the one I love,
> Let him know & finally see
> that the one who loves him is me.
> Keep him Lord keep him 4 Ever.
> But most of all keep us together.
> Amen.

Patricia's "So Young" also talks about love, but we also see the writer raising an issue with which many teenage girls struggle—the issue of whether one should sacrifice female friendship for a man:

I am so young
what should I do
I knew he would never
love me like I wanted him to
it started off just me
then came along Keash and Tresy
we was together for quite a long time
as time went along I wanted to make him all mine
I fought girls to make myself understand.
If I can't have him
nobody can.
He told me he loved me daily
now I found out I am three months pregnant with his baby.
Now I am getting older and am coming to understand
he was never really my man.

Pregnancy is a topic that Patricia continued to explore in an unfinished narrative:

I was mad that day. I had planned to make an appointment to see my doctor. I called the clinic Monday and made an appointment for Saturday, 'cause that was the day she would be at the clinic. I was going to her 'cause I wanted to take a pregnancy test 'cause I had a feeling that I was pregnant. This had been on my mind for about a month and I really wanted to know.

So Saturday came and my appointment was at 2:30 that afternoon and I was so anxious. I had left early from the house so I could be on time. I arrived at the clinic at 2:05. I was early so I got registered at the front desk and signed in and then I went upstairs. When I got upstairs the lady at the desk said she called me to cancel because my doctor wasn't there but I didn't get the call. So she asked if I wanted to go downstairs and do it, and I didn't go up there for nothing so I said yes.

So I went downstairs and the lady told me to pee in the cup and sit in the waiting room and wait to be called on. So I am just sitting there. Then the nurse called me into a room to examine me. She checked my temperature, blood pressure, my weight, and a couple of more things and then she just had me sitting in there to wait on the doctor. So I waited patiently, but scared with all types of things on my mind. . . .

In fact, pregnancy was a common theme for female writers at *La Juventud*, where a significant number of the students were parents. Stories about giving birth and raising children were a way that young women in my writing classes bonded with each other, often writing detailed descriptions of pregnancy, labor, and birth, then reading these descriptions aloud and discussing them with each other. This testifying about one's experiences, particularly experiences that are viewed negatively or simply ignored by the larger society, "is . . . a way to define and redefine one's humanity; to ground oneself in community; to revel in the touch of hands and bodies familiar with the testifier's pain or joy . . ." (Tarpley, 1995, 3). As a woman who has never given birth, I found these conversations fascinating, but I remained an outside observer, much like the young man who was the only male student in one of my writing workshops where many such stories were written and shared.

While the sharing of such stories seemed to me to be a positive thing, enabling teen mothers to feel part of a community, I recall one unexpected issue arising from the sharing of this topic. A student named Julia participated in the conversations, and I had to check with her later to make sure that my memory of what she had previously told me about herself was accurate. The story I remembered was that she had, in fact, given birth to a baby girl about two years previously, but that the baby had been born sick. The baby had stayed in the hospital for awhile, but then Julia insisted on bringing her home, where Julia and her family cared for the infant until she passed away. This was a story that Julia specifically chose not to share with her peers, young women who had in common with her the experience of childbirth, but not her painful aftermath.

This is a useful reminder of the downside of community, which is often rendered in glowingly positive terms. A community is commonly understood as a geographic, social, or psychic space to which certain people belong because of shared histories, interests, or experiences. Yet wherever there is a group of people who belong, there are necessarily others who do not. Gender can be one of the elements that community members share, but it is usually not in itself sufficient. This caveat brings us back to the point I made at the beginning of this chapter, which is that while conversations about gender and literacy can be productive and important, we must approach them with caution, lest we alienate (or re-alienate) young men and women who do not match popular generalizations.

While both Patricia and Marta's writing, above, is about topics connected to sexuality (e.g., romantic relationships, pregnancy), TeTe's writing is the most directly sexual of the female Writers. TeTe's overt approach cannot be separated from her chosen genre—it is no coincidence that she is the only rapper among the females in this book, the only one to use graphic sexual language and imagery, and the only one to write directly about female sexual power.

One powerful way TéTé demonstrates sexual control in her lyrics is through the boast that while she might allow a male to pleasure her, there is a strict line that he is not permitted to cross:

> I ain't that bitch you knew back in elementary school
> I'll get a nigga to eat my clit
> and in return he know he ain't gettin shyt
> these pretty juicy lips ain't used for shyt
> but gettin kissed by a nigga on occasional shyt
> after they do that I know wut you sayin
> a nigga gettin pussy NAW!! they waitin
> no cherry bein popped up in this place
> but I'll pop somethin else up into ya face

What's so interesting about this lyric is the juxtaposition of raw sexuality in vocabulary and description, with a powerful assertion of this woman's refusal to permit actual penetration. The implications of this juxtaposition are various: in a positive sense, it suggests that there is space within the rap discourse to celebrate the power of both female sexuality and virginity, and in a potentially problematic sense, it suggests that female rap writers—even those who don't actually have sex—may see raw sexuality as a required element of their performance.

TéTé does seem to approach the theme of sexual power with relish. Her co-optation of the hypermasculine rhetoric of rap is on prominent display in a freestyle that she wrote to the beat of 50 Cent's 2003 megahit "P.I.M.P." and posted to the Alicia Keys message board. In the original version of the song, a male pimp brags about his work:

> I could care less how she perform when she in the bed
> Bitch hit that track, catch a date, and come and pay the kid . . .

TéTé introduces her version by addressing the other contributors to the message board directly: "Hey y'all, they told me y'all was talkin' about pimpin' and left me out. I can't believe this. I'ma show y'all what true pimpin' is." She goes on to rewrite 50 Cents' intensely masculine boasts, creating a female "P.I.M.P." who can control her 'ho's just as successfully as any man. TéTé apparently has no interest in challenging the fundamental concept of pimping; she does, however, demonstrate the extent to which one can, at least discursively, challenge the parameters of gender-appropriateness simply by claiming a given set of characteristics for oneself:

> I be runnin' shyt constantly
> I be sportin' diamonds and I ain't bought a god dayum thing
> I be havin' niggs strait spendin' they cheese
> and then I'll have the prettiest nigga strait on they knees
> and keep the grimiest strait on the streets so
> he can make that hot young money for me
> now let me tell u about the 1,2,3's of pimpin
>   #1. never ever let a nigga get too close
>   never give em' head
>   never get a nigga who boasts
>   meaning them niggas tell wut ever u do
>   and they'll tell some more even if it's not even true
>   #2. never let a nigga know wut's up
>   never let him know about ya past and who u done cut
>   never let his ass kick it wit ya best friend
>   cuz if they start to catch feelins for 'em u lose a friend
> and #3. the most important rule of these
>   u Never ever, never ever give a nigga some cheese
>   I don't give a fuck if he gives u head galore
>   dump his other chick for u then calls her a whore
>   cuz then a nigga start thinkin' he a pimp
>   then he gon be thinkin' he worth lobster and shrimp . . .

One could choose to read this use of sexuality in a variety of ways. One could, for example, argue that this young woman's confidence in her right to a strong, public sexual persona has feminist overtones. A couple of things keep me from being completely convinced by this reading. One is the line that reads: "Dump his other chick for u then calls her a whore." Assuming that the narrator of the rap sees this act as desirable (if, in this case, not sufficient), the line is bereft of solidarity—the narrator is not concerned about how other women are treated. From this perspective, the subtext of TeTe's response to 50 Cent is, "I'm not one of *those* women. I'm like you." Yet she also says, "never let his ass kick it wit ya best friend/cuz if they start to catch feelin's for 'em u lose a friend," which suggests that the narrator sees her relationships with other women as ultimately more significant than those with men. While I recognize that it's a stretch to draw conclusions based on a few lines in a single rap lyric, TeTe's writing suggests to me that she may be trapped within a common dichotomy: women are either stronger or weaker than men, males are either more or less valuable than females. This is reflected again in the following exchange between TeTe and her friend Stella:

TeTe: [Discussing how she needs to shift her way of thinking when she's giving Stella feedback on a rap] Stella would say something like this, she wouldn't say that, that's more like me, she's more like a lady. I'm more like . . .

Stella: [raising her voice] She's like a man. I'm like feminine.

TeTe: I'm the type of rapper, I'm like a boy, I want you to notice me. And Tete, she like the total opposite of me [referring to her non-rap persona]. I don't usually shout, but Tete, she loud and ghetto and proud of whatever she is [TeTe, Stella, and Jig laugh]. She loud. And she gets anybody's attention, and she said what she said, and you won't understand, or you just won't be able to look.

Again, the equation seems clear: to be "loud and ghetto and proud" is to behave "like a boy," as is the demand for attention and a lack of concern for others' opinions of her.

Listening to TeTe and Stella, I get the sense that there's a negotiation going on among three concepts: lady/feminine, boy/masculine, and a third thing that is as yet unnamed. That third thing, I think, is "woman"—the female who opts out of the discourse of lady-ness. That this term remains unspoken in TeTe's and Stella's conversation could reflect the girls' own lack of clarity about exactly who it is that TeTe is trying to be in her raps, what interests of her own she is trying to serve, and how those interests connect with the gendered identity she is—at age 15—very much in the process of developing. While her lyrics may shock some readers, it is clear that writing gives TeTe a place to wrestle with such questions.

CONCLUSION

In previous chapters, we have seen how the young men and women in this study use imaginative writing to both challenge and reinforce social positioning, to try out a variety of roles, and to connect to family, friends, and admired others. Given the centrality of gender and sexuality to self-image, it is not surprising to find these themes coming up in both overt and covert ways in The Writers' work. The motif of complexity and contradiction that has followed us through earlier chapters is present here as well; through their writing, young women may challenge traditional notions of femininity in one line while reinforcing them in the next, and young men may go from verses that place females clearly below them on the social scale to pieces that acknowledge the particular challenges that women face.

6

"My Work Sparked an Interest in Someone Else"

THE PLEASURES OF IMAGINATIVE WRITING

One of the minor tragedies of extended schooling is that the very things that motivate one to continue formal education after high school sometimes become progressively less alluring as they become progressively more required and evaluated. English majors read less for pleasure during college than they did previously, as they are required to consume and dissect vast amounts of literature on demand. Similarly, the teenage poet who wakes up in the middle of the night with stanzas in her head may lose sight of that passion for composing in the midst of required exercises, drafts, revisions, and critiques from teachers and peers. In the best of worlds, syllabuses and lessons are crafted by professors in ways that make students more, rather than less, excited about the work, and students become more, rather than less, open to previously unexplored genres, styles, and forms. Too often, however, those of us who choose to dedicate ourselves to working with youth and literacy have become distanced from our own early pleasures in the text, and so we forget that we are in the presence of people still in that first flush of excitement over the discovery of new vistas and voices—whether others' or their own. This chapter attempts to demonstrate the various pleasures that The Writers take in their imaginative work, since

> in all the vast body of research and theory on composing that we've generated over the last thirty years or so, none of it addresses that strange, pleasant feeling that sometimes happens

when our writing is going well. This feeling is probably what lured a great many of us to dedicate our intellectual lives to thinking about writing in the first place. (Johnson, qtd. in Skorczewski, 2001, online)

In this chapter, The Writers talk about that in-the-moment pleasurable feeling, but they also talk about the pleasures they take in *having written*—the responses of others to their work, the satisfaction of having crafted a text that does what they wanted it to do, and so on. It is clear that The Writers take deep pleasure in imaginative writing when they are doing it in forms, and for reasons, that matter to them. Pleasure, as The Writers demonstrate, is a powerful motivator, generating attention, engagement, reflection, and learning in ways that we often yearn to see in school.

WHY PLEASURE MATTERS

The writers I worked with experience pleasure-in-writing variously as fun, pride, and satisfaction, and it may be these elements more than anything else that keep them composing. Still, educators may be tempted to see the pleasure of writing as less significant than, say, a text's practical functions or its use as a tool of social critique. Indeed, Roland Barthes (1973) notes that pleasure traditionally has been viewed as something purely personal and conservative in nature:

> An entire minor mythology would have us believe that pleasure (and singularly the pleasure of the text) is a rightist notion. On the right, with the same movement, everything abstract, boring, political, is shoved over to the left and pleasure is kept for oneself . . . On the left, knowledge, method, commitment, combat, are drawn up against 'mere delectation' (and yet: what if knowledge itself were delicious?). On both sides, this peculiar idea that pleasure is simple, which is why it is championed or disdained. (22–23)

Many decades earlier, educational philosopher John Dewey identified a similar phenomenon, using the term "recreation" in ways similar to Barthes' "pleasure":

> I sometimes think that recreation is the most overlooked and neglected of all ethical forces. Our whole Puritan tradition tends to make us slight this side of life, or even condemn it. But the

demand for recreation, for enjoyment just as enjoyment, is one of
the strongest and most fundamental things in human nature.
(Dewey, 2001/1915)

Enjoying what one does seems like an obviously desirable goal—
maybe not one that everyone can always achieve, but certainly one that
would be preferable to being bored or frustrated. But the reality is that
too much enjoyment can cause problems—if too many people start to
demand that work and school become places where they can be intellectually, emotionally, and physically engaged, it could be inconvenient, to
say the least, in sites where efficiency has been highly, even uniquely,
prized. Pleasure takes time—time for creative processes to unfold, time to
experiment and fail and revise and try again, time to linger, to think, to
talk, to share. When teachers, administrators—indeed, whole districts
and states—are focused on raising test scores, that time quickly starts to
seem like a luxury that schools simply cannot afford. Yet, in deciding that
we cannot afford the time that pleasure—that immersion in the processes
of learning—requires, we are, however inadvertently, making a much
larger decision: that we don't believe that different ways of thinking
about, understanding, and engaging with the world are either possible,
useful, or desirable.

The Writers demonstrate that pleasure motivates engagement with
learning, attention to detail, and a desire to excel. It is easy, and at times
useful, to focus on the utilitarian aspects of literacy, either in terms of
conducting everyday exchanges or of exploring the potential of literacy as
a form of democratizing social action. This latter project has been a central area of interest in the last few decades for scholars (Giroux, 1991;
hooks, 1994; McLaren, 2002) building on the work of Paolo Freire (1997
[1970]), who argued that "to speak a true word is to change the world"
(68) and that oppressed peoples could come to verbalize their "true
words" through a process of "conscienticization."[1] Yet focusing on the
ends of literacy risks ignoring the experience itself—that part of writing
that is in excess of immediate practical and political purposes, that part of
textual engagement that Roland Barthes calls pleasure. Barthes defines
pleasure as both an overall category and as the various elements that comprise that category:

On the one hand I need a *general "pleasure"* whenever I must
refer to an excess of the text, to what in it exceeds any (social)
function and any (structural) functioning; and on the other hand
I need a *particular "pleasure,"* a simple part of Pleasure as a whole,
whenever I need to distinguish euphoria, fulfillment, comfort
(the feeling of repletion when culture penetrates freely), from

shock, disturbance, even loss, which are proper to ecstasy, to bliss. (1973, 19, italics added)

We might define Barthes' "general pleasure" as the emotional/intellectual/physical *experience* that writers have in the actual doing of the activity, and that in its purest form manifests itself as creative "flow" (Csikszentmihalyi, 1996): a complete immersion in the moment, often with an accompanying suspension of awareness of physical surroundings and the passage of time. The Writers demonstrate that such pleasure both inspires and enriches learning, in ways that can teach educators much. In the sections that follow, I will offer examples of the "particular pleasures"—the specific *sources* of pleasure—that surface in the talk and the work of The Writers.

SELF-EXPRESSION, REPRESENTATION, AND RESPECT

One source of pleasure becomes apparent when Crazy speaks of the act of creating: "Like a painting, you make something, like an image, and only a certain number of people that see it can understand it." Crazy derives pleasure from the act of creating, but this comment suggests that he also enjoys the control that imaginative writing gives him over who can understand his words and how they understand them. There is a certain thrill in exclusivity—in being a fan of a little-known band, of being invited to join a selective club. Obviously, exclusivity can create huge problems in that people on the inside have a certain power over those who are excluded. My sense is that for Crazy, the pleasure is less one of exclusion than inclusion, as from being able to use writing to externalize his imaginative world in order to draw responses from those for whom that world resonates.

This satisfaction in communicating meaning to an attentive audience is visible in Patricia's words as well: "Like me writing about the [public housing] projects, just telling people how *I* felt about it . . . or what was really behind those buildings, all the dangerousness in them, and me as a child growing up in those projects, what it did to *my* life, how *I* felt about it."

For Patricia, the pleasure of writing comes from the way it allows her to represent herself to others—to reveal her experiences in her own words and her own ways. Robbie writes less about himself; his poetry is often informed by his love of horror movies. "It has to be dark," he told me, referring to the subject matter of his poems. He draws pleasure from crafting his pieces, but as Robbie talks about his first attempts at writing (a story we looked at in Chapter Five as well), it becomes clear that a powerful pleasure for him also lies in the way it makes others respond to him:

> [In eighth grade] a friend told me to write this poem for this girl he liked. I wrote this poem, and he got the girl. And this girl was like, she writes poems, she was the head of the poetry club in his school, and she could swear it was the best poem written by someone. And right now they're gonna get married after high school, and that's my poem, you know? I still hear her recite some of the words.
>
> It was kind of cool, and I thought about it, like, "I'm not around, but my work sparked an interest in someone else." [. . .] That's pretty cool, man, that's what I wanted to see.

Once Robbie realized that he could write things that other people liked, he started writing song lyrics. This was a natural move because of his love of music, but he also hoped that being a songwriter would draw to him the kinds of people who respect rock and roll lyricists:

> [The first song I wrote] was when I was already like fourteen, going into high school. I wrote it in the summer, 'cause I was like, "Hey, man, I'm gonna write a song here, 'cause I know I'm gonna meet some cool people in high school . . ." I'm thinking, "I'm gonna have some songs ready for some people in high school." 'Cause I know when my brother went to high school, he came back with all these artistic people, and I kind of fed off of them a lot, the way they spoke, the way they dressed, the way they were playing their guitar.

Crazy's, Patricia's, and Robbie's comments share an emphasis on relationship—the connection between writer and audience—and on a desire to be understood or to be perceived in a certain way. Patricia's statement, in particular, is all about the pronouns. Her emphasis on the "I/my" makes clear that what's important for her is to tell not the story of *the* projects, but the story of *her* projects—to claim her experience as individual and special, perhaps in unconscious response to the massification of public housing residents through the Discourses of sociological writing and governmental policy statements, and through the flat, anonymous architecture of the physical structures themselves. Patricia reminds us here that being able to name oneself, to tell one's own story, *feels good*. Robbie expresses the pleasure of being praised for what one can create, and the way that pleasure can fuel a continuing desire to develop relation-ships in which a love of various forms of artistic creation can be shared. Crazy, in some ways, combines both of these pleasures.

In Chapter Three, we saw Jig actually separate himself into two identities—Sick Wicked and Jig—in order to experiment with sexually graphic content and then distance himself by commenting, as Jig, on the result. This move allowed Jig to have maximum control over his self-representation and other-perception. It is clear that Jig has a sense of how he wants his audience to perceive him as a writer, and the pleasure that he describes as "fun" in taking on an alternate persona is also a pleasure in having control over exactly who people *think he is* as a writer. This becomes clear when I ask him to explain the difference in the two personas:

> If I'm saying some decent stuff, then that's me as Jig. But if [other freestylers] just said some crazy stuff that don't really mean nothing, then Sick Wicked [responds]; I don't care, just saying something.

If Crazy gets pleasure from eliciting understanding from select others, and Jig gets pleasure from controlling others' perceptions of him, then TeTe's style, as we saw in the last chapter, has at least in part devel-oped out of a sheer desire to be heard. TeTe sees female rappers like Trina and Lil' Kim as models for her own hyper-sexual rhymes. As we have already seen, when I ask her why she chooses sexuality as a primary theme, she explains that it grew out of the fact that she had two older brothers who were already writing and rapping by the time she started out:

> When you grow up and everybody else [is] already doing some-thing, I want to come out and let everybody look at me like, "Man, I'm gonna notice her." And I was the only girl [in The Maniacs] . . . I've always been the youngest, and I'm the only girl, so if I put something out, I want them to be like, "Man, hold on, let me stop and retrace."

TeTe literally wants to make people "stop" and "notice her." Clearly, in an extended family of composers (Mekanismn and the other Maniacs have all been friends of the family so long they might as well be a part of it), being able to use one's words to draw attention away from the rest of the clan is a powerful pleasure for this little sister.

For the writers in this section, one motivation for continuing to compose is that it allows them to manipulate the way that others respond to them; they control how others *see* them by controlling what others *read* and *hear*. They use writing to craft an identity that can be communicated with an audience, and when The Writers sense that they have done that successfully, they experience a pleasure that then motivates them to continue to compose.

DISCURSIVE PLEASURES OF RAP

Among the poets and prose writers in the study—Marta, Patricia, Dave, José, and Robbie—I did not find a strong sense of connection to a particular literary or genre-based tradition. They rarely allude to other writers and texts in their own writing, and they don't cite many literary influences on their own work. That is what makes the clear and conscious connection of the four rappers—Jig, TeTe, Crazy, and Mekanismn—to an artistic community particularly striking, in ways discussed in detail in Chapter Four. There is a particular element of pleasure that comes through again and again as the Maniacs talk about their craft: a deep connection to the rap genre within which they work, and to the larger hip-hop culture of which it is a part. This connection is what makes hip-hop so powerful for youth—they know and care about it because it's *theirs*. They have grown up listening to rap (for many years now the most public element of hip-hop), and that connection between fans' personal histories and the history of the musical form creates a special bond. Mekanismn tells me that he "grew up in" hip-hop, that he is "engrossed in it," that he "lives it": "That's what I do, I'm a hip-hopper. That's what I want to make my life. That's what I want to make my living off, hip-hop music."

The connection that Mekanismn feels with hip-hop generally, and rap specifically, reflects a common emphasis within the Discourse on the conscious awareness of hip-hop as a cultural and historical movement. Representations of hip-hop culture emerged within a decade of DJ Kool Herc's first public use—at Bronx street parties circa 1973—of two turntables to extend the instrumental breaks on old funk and soul records to which Black and Puerto Rican "b-boys" (the "b" comes from "break") performed their increasingly rhythmic, gymnastic, and gravity-defying moves. In 1982, the movie *Wild Style* "feature[ed] the first full-length account of all four elements in hip hop culture" (B-Boys.com), publicly announcing hip-hop as a coherent and thriving youth movement.

Rap, specifically, has a strong tradition of self-reference, intertextuality, and attention to the history of the musical genre and to the larger hip-hop culture. Crazy follows this genre-referencing discursive model in the following freestyle:

> How many ya'll know how to kill beats
> Without having to breathe deep
> Surpassed Jay-Z's class
> Lost myself
> But I found me in stealth
> Purple pills
> Will just slow myself
> Until my invasion
> Released like I dropped 50
> But I'd rather place an X
> Just to Detonate and Massacre . . .

Here, Crazy has some fun formulating rhymes around references to rappers Jay-Z, Eminem, 50 Cent, and DMX. While some of the references are obvious, like the overt mentions of Jay-Z and 50, the others require specific knowledge. Eminem is alluded to twice: "lost myself" is a play on the Detroit rapper's Academy Award-winning song "Lose Yourself," and "Purple Pills" is the title of a song by Eminem's group, D12. And while I did catch on to the DMX reference in "I'd rather place an X" (I know that DMX is a favorite rapper of both Crazy and Jig, and that he is sometimes referred to simply as "X"), it took me a few reads to pick up on the fact that the letter "X" is followed by the capitalized words "Detonate" and "Massacre." Put the three capital letters together and you have . . . DMX. Crazy's decision to incorporate allusions to a number of popular artists in a freestyle about his own experience and skills reflects the intensity of his identification with the artists and texts that comprise the genre. The imaginative way he carries out the project demonstrates the *pleasure* he takes from in-group textual play that, by definition, only participants in the rap Discourse can fully appreciate.

Clearly, rap is a much more popular and in some ways accessible (because of its more familiar language and its ubiquity in the media) genre than, say, poetry or fiction for U.S. teenagers and young adults. So it makes sense that young rappers would be especially immersed in their artistic community. But rap also has a strong tradition of self-reference, intertextuality, and attention to the history of the genre—as young fans see such preoccupations in the work of their favorite artists, they simultaneously internalize these approaches to writing.

Two connected examples illustrate the kinds of generic homage that developing rappers hear. First, there are the allusions to early hip-hop media in Notorious B.I.G.'s hit "Juicy" (1994):

> I used to read *Word Up* magazine, Salt 'n' Pepa and Heavy D up
> in the limousine/ . . . every Saturday Rap Attack, Mr. Magic,
> Marley Marl . . .[2]

Mos Def pays a double homage in his song "Love" (1999b), in which he reminds us of Biggie's lines while simultaneously namechecking Rap Attack and its host:

> In '83, Benny C was the host with the most
> I listened to the Rap Attack and held the radio close . . .[3]

In addition to providing models of generic allusion for young rappers, lyrics like Biggie's and Mos Def's read as a timeless description of the young rap fan/writer; both songs create a connection between the successful rapper and the kid sitting in his/her room, listening to a favorite CD and scribbling in a cheap notebook—"I was you," they seem to be saying, in a message that reinforces the young fan/writer's sense of artistic community.

As Mos Def's "Love" continues, it expresses the deep connection young people have to their music while offering a description of the rap version of "flow":

> When you close your eyes and screw your face, is this the pain
> of too much tenderness
> To make me nod my head in reverence . . .

Here again, the successful and respected rapper presents himself as the young fan and developing writer, similar to those in the present study.

What I find particularly interesting as I reread the lyrics to "Love" is the way Mos Def describes both listening and writing as intensely physical activities. He "held the radio close"; he says that "you close your eyes and screw your face"; he *felt* pain, *nodded* his head . . . This seems to me to be yet one more element of pleasure in writing—it is *embodied* creation. Part of "being in the moment" is being in one's body—being fully intellectually, emotionally, and physically caught up. Crazy and Jig reflect this physicality in their descriptions of writing: in the next section, Crazy describes rap "battles" as akin to schoolyard play, and Jig illustrates the extent to which creative flow can alter normal physical responses (such as not going to the bathroom once during a six-hour competition with a friend). This is yet another important aspect of creative work that is unattended to in traditional classrooms—if one is effectively immobilized in one's chair, the chances of getting carried away by one's work are lessened.

PLAY

> By not acknowledging the deep visceral pleasures black youth derive from making and consuming culture, the stylistic and aesthetic conventions that render the form and performance more attractive than the message, [scholars] reduce expressive culture to a political text to be read like a less sophisticated version of *The Nation* or *Radical America*.
>
> —Kelley, 1997, 37

Finally, there is the sense of pleasure in play—the element of sheer fun. As Jig does earlier in this chapter, Crazy specifically uses the word *fun* to characterize the feeling of being in a rap battle:

> Oh, it's fun, it's almost like you're a kid all over again, talking about somebody, like you back in elementary, bringing back the kid inside, it's just fun . . . I don't take it serious. I just know that they're trying to make me get mad. Like me being a kid again, like I can keep poking you just to try and get you mad [he mimics a child's mocking tone]: "I'm not touching you, I'm not touching you."

Crazy explicitly equates fun with being a child, suggesting that there is an innocence to play that allows one to get away with certain kinds of behavior that might be read differently outside of the playground—literally, the *ground* set aside for *play*, the ground on which everything that occurs is understood as play. This is significant given that battle-rap is founded on play-transgression, much like The Dozens, the traditional African-American oral form of verbal insult-play most commonly known as the source of "yo' momma" jokes. Off the playground, an insult to someone's "momma" is dangerous indeed; but on the playground—whether the jointly recognized ground of The Dozens or of battle rap—"yo' momma," and everything else, is fair game. This is exactly because the message is never really about anyone's actual "momma," but about "the humor, the creative pun, the outrageous metaphor" (Kelley, 1997, 34).

Winnicott (1971, 48) suggests that the earliest manifestations of play in infants are directly connected to trust—in fact, he says, "playing implies trust" (51). I extrapolate from this that the level of play possible between individuals is directly related to the level of trust in their relationship. Take, for example, Jig, TeTe, and Crazy's description of a marathon rap battling session Jig engaged in with a friend:

SW: How long will you guys go for?

Jig: I think one time . . .

Crazy [yelling over from the computer]: SIX HOURS.

TeTe: Six hours straight [all laugh].

Jig: We were freestyling. He said something about me; we just went back and forth, until like seven in the morning.

SW: Did you go to the bathroom?

Jig: We wouldn't even sit down, we were just standing up going back and forth . . .

Stella (TeTe's friend): Nothing to drink?

Jig: You don't even think about it. It's just that moment, the whole world changes, it's just you and that person.

Crazy: Like in *The Matrix*.

TeTe: Like you in the rap matrix.

Jig: Your thoughts come a lot easier; everything comes a lot easier . . . you'll start going into your zone; that's the only thing you see at the moment. Everything starts to work a lot easier, a lot quicker.

The centrality of trust and comfort to this kind of deep play might explain why Jig and his friend can happily "battle" for six hours, lost in pure flow. These two young men have known each other for years; they have developed their rapping and writing skills together; they both understand that their play battles are just that—play—and that what sound like attacks on the surface in fact represent a deep affinity. The lack of such a history and established camaraderie would also explain why public rap battle events follow established routines, such as set time limits and clearly identified rules for naming winners[4]—explicit rules are required where trust cannot be assumed. Finally, the connection between play and trust can help us to understand why rap battles sometimes have nothing to do with play, and everything to do with real, and often really dangerous, aggression, as illustrated in the discussion about Tupac Shakur and Biggie Smalls in Chapter Two. This is a useful lesson for the classroom—if teachers are going to make space for play, including playful competition, it is important that clear guidelines be established—at least until students and teacher all come to know and trust one another.

When such trust, respect, and/or rules exist, the pleasure of rapping is often that it creates an arena for individuals to play with roles that would not normally be either available or appropriate to them. TeTe demonstrates this when she talks about her rap persona, as we saw in Chapter Five (TeTe is her rap name, not her real name):

> I'm the type of rapper, I'm like a boy, I want you to notice me. And TeTe, she like the total opposite of me, I don't usually shout . . . but TeTe, she loud and ghetto and proud of whatever she is [laughs]. And she gets anybody's attention, and she said what she said, and you won't understand, or you just won't be able to look [. . .] You're like, "Ooooo," or I'll try to chew somebody up, and everybody be like, "Ooooo."

By playing her rap persona against her everyday identity, TeTe is able to draw a response from her audience that adds to her pleasure. Play provides a site where she can safely play at transgressing the rules of gender. As Rose points out,

> by paying close attention to female rappers, we can gain some insight into how young African-American women provide for themselves a relatively safe *free-play* zone where they creatively address questions of sexual power, the reality of truncated economic opportunity, and the pain of racism and sexism. (1994, 146, italics added)

TeTe uses rap in quite conscious ways to play at different ways of "doing" sexuality and aggression in front of an audience that implicitly understands that it *is* play—a performance that they are not to take literally or expect her to live up to once she leaves the (literal or figurative) stage.

The fact that play suspends the normal rules of propriety lets rappers—and freestyle battlers in particular—extend the limits of what would normally be acceptable content. Like TeTe and other female rappers, male rappers draw heavily on themes of sexuality and gender. In both cases, there are countless examples of the reinscription of stereotypical roles—male rappers brag about the number of women they bed and their ability to avoid commitment to a single female, while female rappers foreground their sexuality through revealing clothing and either boast of their own sexual skills or criticize the shortcomings of other women. Yet like TeTe, Jig is able to try on attitudes alien to his everyday behavior when playing with rap. In an interview about rap writing, he gleefully recounted to me the following stories:

> *Jig*: There was a [local] rapper named Eydea [pronounced "Idea"]. He was battling somebody, and they had on some red jogger pants. He said—and it was a dude—he said, "I can tell you're a female/you about to be killed/your pants used to be white/until your period spilled."
>
> *Jig*: And the more that you know a person [the more effectively you can battle them], 'cause you need to draw on all that stuff at the moment. One of my friends tried to say something about me, and I know him real well, and I know his girlfriend is white, so I'm like, "I already know your girl/you ought to keep her in place/she used to be black/until I came on her face."

How to explain the apparent contradiction between Jig's everyday character and his enjoyment of—and creation of—what many would see as overtly misogynistic rhymes? Part of the answer lies in the question itself—it's that very disjunction between reality and the fantasy of play that makes clearly "politically incorrect" themes so effective. As Jig explains, "Normally freestyling like that isn't a representation of who you truly are. Needless to say I ain't turned no Black girls White." Remember, in a freestyle battle, the opponents are responding to one another but also playing to the audience, which has the ultimate say over who wins and who loses. Saying things that one is not supposed to say is one powerful way to get the audience's attention. Saying something completely out of character is another. And one of the most effective strategies in battle rap is to use what one knows about an opponent against him or her (the final battle scene in *8 Mile* is a striking example of this technique).

The other explanation goes right back to that issue of trust as a requirement of deep play. Jig knew the person he was battling against well, and also knew the girlfriend he references in his rhyme:

> I only said it because we were stating stuff that we knew about each other. He said something about the girl I was with at the time, and I came back at him with that. Me and his girl was cool anyway, and we played like that sometimes, when all of us were together, although we might not play like that with everyone. It was something we was cool with.

In other words, she knew that Jig was safe—not a threat to her, not someone who actually looked at her that way. That mutual understanding—that trust—made it okay for him to refer to her in play the way that he did. As far as why such themes and tactics play so well with audiences of both genders, Jig says, "Some think it's funny because it's just music, and in music you're not always yourself, no matter what the music is. When you do opera or whatever they train you to become a different person when you're onstage and to break out of character when you're not performing. And some people understand that."

The way Jig, TeTe, and Crazy tell it, the whole point of rap battling is to provide maximum pleasure for both the performers and the audience. When I ask how they can gauge the audience's appreciation, they answer by *becoming* the audience—by performing the audience's reactions:

> *TeTe*: It makes people, like, "Ooooo." If you on the floor and
>   you can make everybody like, "oooo," you wonderful.
> *SW*:   Can you tell the difference between when people think it's
>   just okay and when they're blown away by it?
> *Jig*:   Yeah. They'll get more elaborate with it. [On the Alicia
>   Keys message board] Instead of saying, "That's cool,"
>   they'll write a whole lot more, like "It made me think of
>   such and such . . ."
> *TeTe*: [Or they'll say] "Oh my *god*, that was *ignorant!*" ["Igno-
>   rant" in this case being a very good thing, since it suggests
>   that one has gotten in a powerful dig at one's opponent.]

Winnicott tells us that parts of playing involve unrelated thought sequences—what might look like nonsense to an observer. "Free association that reveals a coherent theme is already affected by anxiety, and the cohesion of ideas is a defence [sic] organization" (1971, 55–56). It is striking to me how close Jig's description of freestyle rap is to this definition; he says that when one is in the middle of a freestyle session, "your state of conscious thought over what you are saying is gone." While I don't believe that Winnicott's psycho-therapeutic view of play-as-free-association maps exactly onto the current topic of play-in-composition (especially as "cohesion of ideas" is implicit in the very definition of most kinds of composition—from freestyle raps to doctoral dissertations), it is useful to consider that a premature emphasis on form, structure, and organization in classroom activities related to writing may eliminate the possibility for students to play with new ideas—to be deeply creative. When teachers get cookie-cutter essays with predictable topics, organization, and transitions ("first/second/finally"; "conversely"; "in conclusion"), it is either because that is what they have directly requested or because the students have not had the time, space, or tools for initial play with the material. Either that, or—to use Winnicott's terminology—the students have developed an anxiety about schooling that causes every assignment and activity to be carried out "defensively," in a way that is safe enough to get them by and to protect them from embarrassment, humiliation, censure, or failure.

CONCLUSION

Given the current emphasis on quantitative measurement as both the format and the goal of education, teachers may worry that attention to students' pleasure in the process of learning is a luxury that they simply cannot afford. They may also worry about how such attention could be perceived:

> Sometimes people assume that if the teacher is interested in pleasure, then he or she must be very lax with regard to teaching the conventions that enable successful communication. That is, people locate pleasure in a hazy binary with discipline, and then assume that our pedagogic mission has nothing to do with the former and everything to do with the latter. (Johnson, qtd. in Skorczewski, 2001, online)

Yet what The Writers have demonstrated is that pleasure motivates engagement with learning, attention to detail, and a desire to excel. It is also (and here is where things get controversial) an end in itself. Imagine, you teachers, researchers, and other readers, if you were daily discouraged from reading the things you enjoy, from listening to the music you love. Imagine if you were judged and evaluated on each idea you voiced in the midst of an impromptu conversation, in the midst of what we adults describe as "thinking aloud" (it suddenly strikes me that only spelling separates that phrase from "thinking allowed"). Imagine if someone followed you around, telling you which of the poets you love "counts" as a writer.

Pleasure is a quality-of-life issue. It is also a quality-of-learning issue. For several of The Writers, the kind of learning that involves taking risks, trying new things without worrying about getting everything just right, and pushing oneself past previous knowledge and accomplishments, looks a lot like play,[5] pride, enjoyment—like pleasure. "Learning," in other words, "should be 'hard fun' that leads to immediate and significant satisfactions" (Wilhelm, qtd. in NCTE, 2004, online), to pleasure in each step of the process, rather than to a sole focus on the outcome.

All of the voices we've heard in this chapter suggest that acts of oral
and written composition are meaningful when they elicit a response from
the writer, and when that response and the writing itself occur simultaneously—when one *feels things* about the writing as one writes. Over and
over again, The Writers say that—far from having to make themselves
write, as so many students at all levels of formal education seem to—they
are regularly overtaken by an impulse, a desire, a drive to compose:

> *Marta*:   [The words] just pop out, they just pop up in my
>   mind, and I write them down.
> *Mekanismn*: Basically [if] I'm at home or somewhere and I get a
>   thought, pop into my head, stay in your head . . .
>   Even if it's like, something long, either I keep it in
>   my head or I just jot it down real quick, so I can
>   have it for later on.
> *Dave*:   I'll be taking a shower, and an idea will come to me,
>   and I'll have to run out and write it down before I
>   forget, and then finish it off. Driving, it's probably
>   worse than talking on a cell phone, 'cause I'm trying
>   to write—I don't want to lose the idea.

I don't expect that any amount of restructuring in our understandings
of writing will result in everyone running around with odes on their fore-
arms, as Dave sometimes does when he has no paper on which to scribble
a sudden verse. Different people use different forms as creative outlets.
But an emphasis on the immediate and extended pleasures of learning,
rather than on the results of having learned, would make for a different
kind of classroom, one in which students move around, work with one
another and with the teacher, sometimes stay after class because they
want to keep working, and see less of a distinction between school work
and the "real" thing.

7

"I'm Book Smart, Street Smart & Everything in Between"

WRITING, LITERATE IDENTITY, AND ACADEMIC ACHIEVEMENT

Look at me, still in school with a 4.0
3 years of college, went from poetry, to the kid with the magnificent flow
i'm super literate, some even consider me genius
i'm book smart, street smart, and everything in between it's
miraculous, nothing short of spectacular
depending on the situation i can switch my vernacular
if i don't believe in me, then who the fuck will
who would shed a tear at my funeral if tomorrow i was suddenly killed
if i don't impact a life, then i ain't rhymin' for shit
I spit on a level that everyone can cop with
associate they life with
that's why when you read it, you get the image in yo' optics
I can flow on different topics
no matter what, i automatically drops it
listen to my songs, you get extra wrinkles in yo' brain
who said rap ain't educational, play 'em a track from Jig Insane.

— —

> People do not just do writing. They have ideas in their mind
> about what it means to do it. (Sheridan et al., 2000, 109)

— —

The last bar of Jig's rhyme, above, does two things simultaneously—happily for us, the very two things that are the subject of this chapter. On the one hand, his "who says rap ain't educational/play 'em a track from Jig Insane" suggests that the lyric itself is an educational text, that Jig's listeners will learn something by attending to his rhymes. At the same time, it is a declaration of Jig's intelligence and a description of some of the elements of communication that he's both learned and refined through his rap writing. He says that "depending on the situation i can switch my vernacular," and that

> I spit on a level that everyone can cop with
> associate they life with
> that's why when you read it, you get the image in yo' optics
> I can flow on different topics

Jig exhibits through these lyrics a consciousness of audience, of imagery, of versatility, and of communicative competence across diverse contexts. In this chapter, we will look specifically at how and what The Writers learn through their composing practices and through participation in text-centered Discourses.

THE EDUCATOR'S DILEMMA

Every once in awhile, I stumble across an article, song, or statement that crystallizes a concept I've been trying to verbalize for months. Such was the case when a former student in one of my university methods classes forwarded me an article from *Rethinking Schools* called "The Politics of Correction." My student wrote, "This reminded me of what you taught us":

> These days, I'm frequently called into schools to "fix" students' grammar and punctuation errors. I admit to feeling churlish about using conventions—punctuation, grammar, spelling—as the entry point to student writing. I believe writing must begin in students' lives and be generated for real audiences. However, in recent years I've witnessed too many low-income students, students of color, and immigrant students who have not learned how to use Standard English—the language of power.
>
> Sure they can write great slam poetry; some can even write killer stories; a few can write essays, but they are often riddled with convention errors. Failing to learn these skills handcuffs students. Their lack of fluency with the language of power will

follow them like the stench of poverty long after students leave school—silencing them by making them hesitant to speak in public meetings or write their outrage over public policy because they "talk wrong."

So how do we both nurture students in their writing and help them learn the language of power? (Christensen, 2003, ¶ 3–4)

On the one hand, I was gratified that my emphasis on what I consider a central issue in teaching English to secondary students had stuck with the person who sent me this article. Like Christensen, I "believe writing must begin in students' lives and be generated for real audiences." On the other hand, one sentence mocked me: "Sure they can write great slam poetry; some can even write killer stories; a few can write essays, but they are often riddled with convention errors." I was aware of this tension, of course, but I had also spent the last year or two focusing quite a lot on those imaginative poems, stories, and essays, and celebrating the skills and talents of their writers.

I had, however, also recently responded to a plea from one of the writers in this book to help him with an essay for his college English class. Troubled by his lack of ability to incorporate quotations from a novel into an essay in a coherent way, I wrote the following to my advisor:

I went over to –'s today to help him with a literature paper for a class he's taking at City College. Very interesting, and a useful reminder of how much the out-of-school writing does NOT pre-pare students for academic writing . . .

I do not intend to offer "the solution" to this dilemma, for one simple reason: I don't have it. I don't have it for another simple reason: It doesn't exist. Every experienced teacher knows that there is no such thing as a foolproof curriculum; the lesson plan that works phenomenally first period might bomb during third. In addition, as we've seen throughout this book, the tensions and disconnections described above are less about classrooms and schools than they are about American society and cul-ture(s) writ large. Within the context of the quite complicated matrix of race, gender, and class that infuses questions of language, literacy, and education, there are nonetheless classrooms around the country where the complexities are negotiated in productive ways. These sites have been documented in a number of articles and books (Morrell and Duncan-Andrade, 2002; Lee, 1993; Mahiri, 1998). It is not the purpose of this chapter, or this book, to add to that important work of documentation. I do think it's important to emphasize, though, that all such approaches take place in specific, local environments and involve actual people who— together, and only together—make them work.

Having said that, what this chapter *will* do is clarify just what is going on, composition-wise, in rap ciphers,[1] rhyme books, and young writers' talk about their work. To value a practice without really understanding it is, after all, of limited use. The other chapters in this book challenge readers to value youths' imaginative writing by demonstrating how and why the writing matters. This chapter examines—in terms of learning models, writing processes and literary and stylistic elements—how this writing comes to be.

COGNITIVE APPRENTICESHIP

The major learning model that The Writers use is cognitive apprentice- ship. Briefly, I define cognitive apprenticeship as an educative process involving a relative novice and a relative expert in a given Discourse. In cognitive apprenticeship, as in traditional apprenticeships, "learners can see the processes of work" (Collins, et al. 1991) as they are performed by skilled practitioners of that work; learners develop their own abilities by practicing the work with less and less guidance until they are confident and competent to do it on their own. One of the key markers of a healthy apprenticeship model is an understanding (overt or implicit) among all participants that the novice and expert are both invested in the Discourse in question, and that both have a vested interest in the interaction.

To my way of thinking, the ideal educative relationship involves shift- ing learning models and roles—sometimes there is a clear novice and a clear expert; sometimes the same two participants might be collabora- tively engaged in developing a new skill or understanding; sometimes the novice in one situation becomes the expert in another; and so on. Recog- nizing this fluidity of roles and learning models creates a healthy instabil- ity, such that no single person can assume that he/she is always or should always be in charge, and no single person is automatically and always sub- ordinate. This fluidity is a marker of many of the educative interactions I documented and/or heard about in my research.

In Chapter Four, we saw a version of cognitive apprenticeship in the way that Crazy and TeTe have been inspired by—and continue to learn from—their older brother Jig's writing, and how Crazy has taken on that same role for younger sister TeTe. TeTe is now carrying on this tradition by helping her friend Stella develop her own skills as a lyricist:

Stella: I write rap, a little bit, but I'm more into my poetry. Like I'm learning now, I'm in the learning process of writing lyrics.

TeTe: She comin' out. She'll have a rap or something laid out, and then she'll bring it to me, or bring it to Crazy or somebody, and we'll read over it, and we're like, "Okay, that's tight, but you flow it like this." Or, "Why don't you find a flow and put it in, and change this . . . cut that line short, take out this word, and put this word."

I have found evidence of cognitive apprenticeship not only among The Writers, but among other participants on the Keys website. While following the thread daily as part of my research with the Maniacs, I came upon an exchange by Sim and Ambishn, two frequent contributors to the thread, that crystallized something for me about rap and learning by displaying an early step in the cognitive apprenticeship model. In the following example, Sim presents herself as someone who wants to learn about freestyling from people whom she views as skilled practitioners. Sim has already read the writing of the people she names; here, Ambishn acts as the expert to Sim's apprentice as he explains how that writing is constructed and what features matter in judgments of its quality:

Sim: MAAAAAAADDDD propz to ya all!! Dat includes
          Ambishn, Kimistry, Tor, Jig, Unavailable . . .
          and all da others!!!! I live in da UK, so there
          ain't much freestyling. I'm really interested .
          . . can u guys do this on da spot . . . like
          rap it or do u write it down first?

Ambishn: Well, freestyle is a gift, not anyone can just
          flip it off the top of the head. These rhymes
          we all wrote . . . most of all of them were
          freestyle. All of mine are. But regardless from
          freestyle and written, it's the vision and
          depth that makes it hot!! It don't have to be
          on spot, well . . . unless you're tested by a
          MC [in hip-hop parlance, an MC is a rapper].
          That's when most likely it's freestyle cause
          you have to rip it quick. But thank you soo
          much for the compliment. I appreciate it and I
          know they all do too! =) Stay up Sim. (2003)

The lens of discourse analysis is useful in understanding Sim and Ambishn's exchange here, in that it provides helpful insights into the way that two young people interested in a particular genre of writing cooper-ate to construct and then interact within a cognitive apprenticeship model. In Sim's and Ambishn's exchange we can clearly identify the role each person agrees to occupy in relation to the other. Sim begins by fore-grounding her novice standing through a rhetorical bow to the most pro-lific writers on the site. She gives these writers mad propz—in current usage, *mad* means *large amounts of* (as in, "he's making mad money at that job") and *propz* or *props* translates to *credit* or *praise* (as in, "I give you props for even trying to read that book"). Not only does Sim give the writers on the message board mad propz, but she capitalizes and multi-plies the *A*s and *D*s in *mad* for extra emphasis.

Sim transitions from the initial move of overt praise into her purpose for writing, which is to get information about freestyling. She does this through a sentence that offers both an explanation for and another acknowledgement of her novice status—a status that she extends (perhaps unfairly) to her entire country by saying, "I live in da UK, so there ain't much freestyling."

However, Sim simultaneously attempts to mediate her low-status self-inscription by demonstrating that while she may be on the outside in terms of knowing the rules of freestyle, she is a cultural insider. We are tipped off to this through the self-conscious use of both youth slang and African American Vernacular English (AAVE). Sim signals her familiarity with youth culture discourse through use of the already-discussed phrase *mad propz*, as well as by using the idiosyncratic spelling (in both *propz* and in the repeated use of the letter *u* in place of *you*) that marks hip-hop orthography (Olivo, 2001). Sim also asserts insider status by incorporat-ing a common feature of AAVE pronunciation—replacing the *th* clusters at the beginnings of words with *d*s. Interestingly, Sim doesn't do this at every opportunity; note the inconsistency in these lines: "I live in *da* UK, so *there* ain't much freestyling. I'm really interested . . . can u guys do *this* on *da* spot . . .". This could be read as consistency in inserting the *d* only for the word *the*, except that Sim *does* replace the *th* with *d* in *that/dat* in her second sentence.

Ambishn, conversely, represents his expert status not only through the content of his response, but also by assuming the right to speak for the board as a whole: "these rhymes *we all* write," "I appreciate it and *I know they all do too!*" Notably, his language usage also appears to be less self-conscious. There is some use of slang, but there are no variations from standardized grammar or spelling.

This brief analysis demonstrates the extent to which the participants in this conversation, representing fairly typical members on this message board, are powerfully—if unconsciously—adept at taking on the learning and teaching roles that are so often a part of the educative process. Both Sim and Ambishn accept these roles and willingly enact them for their mutual benefit—Sim gains greater understanding of freestyle rapping, and Ambishn experiences the pleasure both of praise from an appreciative audience member and of performing the role of expert in a Discourse he obviously values.

Just as young poets' and rappers' eagerness to engage in writing outside of the classroom is often in direct contradiction to their reception of writing instruction in school, Sim's and Ambishn's easy enactment of cognitive apprenticeship suggests that young people do, in fact, want to learn from more experienced others, much as professional educators may sometimes feel that they don't. The difference here is the difference between the traditional hierarchical teacher/learner interaction and the cognitive apprenticeship model, in which the learner takes an active role by observing the work of a skilled practitioner, asking questions, and practicing with the skilled other's guidance. In this model, the novice is not required to take on faith the teacher's expertise; instead, she actually gets to observe the expert's craft firsthand—something that is often not the case in the standard classroom, where students may be taught writing by a teacher whose own writing they've never seen. It is also understood from the beginning that the goal is for the novice to become an expert in her own right, and that the roles that the participants inhabit will therefore shift over time. Finally, goals and desired outcomes are identified from the outset, so the learner knows why she is engaging with the work—and in this case at least, has fully chosen this engagement for herself.

THE WRITING PROCESS

Whether The Writers work in rap or in more traditional forms like poetry, their comments make clear that they act *as writers*. They clearly verbalize and analyze the various elements of their form, and they talk to one another not just as friends but as fellow composers who can teach and learn from one another. The amount of time, effort, and concentration they put into working on a piece of writing, and on generally developing their skills, can be striking, as Moje (2000) noted in her work with gang-connected adolescents:

> As I watched [them] use literacy, I was intrigued with the contradiction I saw between their motivation to rapidly internalize very specific and complicated gang writing styles, spellings, rules, and

dress codes, and their seeming indifference to using conventional
writing styles, spellings, punctuation, and grammars. (652)

The Writers are not necessarily "indifferent" to academic conventions.
They do not, however, see such conventions as more important than
writing's communicative function. The extent to which young people
interpret school as privileging the more superficial aspects of composition
may be the extent to which they do not engage in the classroom.

In describing her writing process, Patricia says that she tends to draft
and revise simultaneously. When she has a version that she likes, she
requests critical feedback from a cousin who is attending one of the local
city colleges. This cousin offers specific comments, which I would often
see written on the pages of the writing Patricia showed to me in class. In
fact, for a while I thought that she was showing me work that she had
already handed in to another teacher because the comments looked so
"teacherly":

> My cousin'll be like, "Yeah, you should put that part in front of
> that part," or "you should change this" or "talk about this." And
> he'll say that, too [she points to her son's father, sitting on the
> couch], like before when I was writing about the projects, he's
> like, "Well, you should add this," 'cause, like, telling how the
> projects really was. "You should add this, or you should add
> that." That's how I get a lot of opinions. And a lot of poems
> when I write and I read my writing . . . I be wanting to write it
> different. If I start writing it over, I want to change something.
> So I write something totally different. So, that's how I be (small
> laugh) . . . I'm like "Oh, I forgot this"; the second time I write, I
> be like, "Yeah, let me write this," or "change this word," or "put
> this in front of this word." That's how I do most of the time.

It seems that when young people have some sense of control over the
means of learning, they are not only willing but eager to accept criticism:

> SW: It's usually hard to have people make suggestions—
> Stella: —'cause it hurts.
> SW: Right, even if you know that it'll be better.
> TeTe: If I want something to be right, I'm gonna ask the person.
>   Like my writing, [if] I want it to be right, I'm gonna go
>   ask Jig. I'm gonna be like, "Jig, how this sound?" And Jig
>   be like, "Put this here, change it change it change it . . ."
>   And it's cool.

Jig: I'm not like telling them, "You have to do this." I just give
        her suggestions, and they'll say, "Well, maybe this, that
        . . . Yeah, that sounds good."
SW: Do you sometimes not take his suggestions?
TeTe: I take his suggestions [laughs]. They turn out to be right.

As useful as receiving criticism by respected others is for the apprentice writer, the act of formulating feedback is just as effective at helping
more experienced composers learn how to critique without taking over a
piece of writing:

Jig: If somebody comes to me for suggestions, I'm going to do
        it according to how *they* rap, so you wouldn't even be able
        to tell that I had anything to do with it. You'd think it was
        them.
SW: How do you know how to do that?
Jig: I'm able to put myself inside of somebody else's shoes.
        Instead of it constantly being my way, I can look at things
        from another person's perspective. Like . . . if I was them,
        this is how I would say it.

To be fair, not every young writer is quite so open to criticism. Stella,
above, acknowledges that it can be a "hurtful" process, though one she is
trying to open up to. When I was first getting to know Marta, as a student in my writing workshop at *La Juventud*, she resisted my suggestion
to get feedback for revision from another student in the class. She
explained that she had worked really hard on the poem in question to get
it this way, that she had written and crossed out and rewritten when she
worked on it the previous night, and that now she was happy with it and
didn't want to change it. The key here was for both of us to recognize
that she *can* accept criticism—her own, or sometimes, as she later told
me, her mother's. From there, it became easier for me to occasionally be
less, well, pushy about revision, and for us to start talking about the
potential usefulness of considering others' takes on her writing.

DEVELOPING CRAFT

While a number of The Writers expressed occasional hesitation to alter
their words or what they saw as the style that made their writing unique,
all of them showed evidence of crafting—thinking about, drafting, and
reworking—their pieces. The extent to which they do this depends on the

genre in which they're writing and what their purpose is. Even within a single Discourse, there are differences in how one crafts particular kinds of texts, as Jig demonstrates in explaining how the process of writing song lyrics differs from that of freestyling:

> When you're trying to form a song together, when you have a beat to it, then you can't just say everything as soon as it comes into your mind—that's more like a freestyle. If you're forming a song, you got to find different words that fit better than other words. Like sometimes, even me, sometimes when I rap it, there's certain things that it's harder for me to say, because of the way that I talk. I could slur some words, and then it's harder to understand, so I switch some lyrics. Sometimes I'll run a lot of words together, but some words just don't come out of my mouth as good and don't sound as good . . . I don't just go ahead and automatically change it. I could try to write a different type of lyric to get it out better. If I can do that, I'll just leave it alone. Like sometimes, I have to slow down a certain part, and speed up the next thing, to keep it on the same beat. And some words just don't have to be there, some words [are] just filler and just take up space.

Like Jig, José talks about the way that approaches to revision grow out of necessity. Lacking Jig's relatively stable personal and educational history (*relatively* being an important term here, since Jig's family has had its share of financial and emotional struggles), José has had little more than his own eyes and ears to follow in revising his work. The impact of cognitive apprenticeship is evident by its absence in José's experience. Without the guidance of more experienced writers in his genre-of-choice, José has at times abandoned writing that he could not fashion to his own satisfaction:

> I can't write perfect. Like you [he indicates me], you proba- bly could write very good, but like the punctuation, the periods, I'm not good at that 'cause I was never taught how to do it . . . When I was in Audi home [the Chicago home for juvenile criminal offenders], I would write how I think is right. People would tell me that it don't make sense, but I knew in my mind that it makes sense for me because I wrote it.
>
> *SW*: So how would you figure out what was right?
>
> *José*: Well, I'll read it a couple times and write it a couple of times. If I write something right now and I read it and it

don't look right to me, I'll throw it away. People say I
shouldn't do it, [that] I should finish writing it, and then
write it over, and then look at it, summarize it and then do
it over again. But for me, if I start something like, "Hi my
name," and it doesn't sound right, I'll rip up the page.

SW: Now do you just give up on that idea, or start over with the
same idea?

José: Like, if I'm writing a short story, I'll come up with the same
idea 'cause it's still in my head. I'll write it down very, very
fast so I don't forget it. I'll have it written down, because I
really want to concentrate on what I'm writing on that. If I
write on something else it's gonna block out my memory,
and I'm not gonna remember what I wanted to write about,
and then later on it's gonna bother me, like, "Why didn't I
write that instead of this?"

As I related near the beginning of this book, my introduction to José's
poetry actually came through his girlfriend Flor, who showed me several
typed copies of his poems that she had in her school binder. It seems that
having a significant other to write for and to share writing with has made
a difference in the value that José puts on his own work. He tells me that
most of what he wrote in the Audi home was about his family—a difficult topic, to be sure—and so it didn't much bother him when his suitcase, with all of that work inside, was stolen. Now, though, Flor either
directly or indirectly inspires much of his poetry, and her valuing of it
and him seems to have affected his own sense of its importance. What's
striking to me is that Dave tells a similar story, as we saw in Chapter
Three: for several years, he wrote poetry in notebooks and on scraps of
paper, only to throw it away when he was done. He didn't start saving his
work until a cousin found one of his notebooks, "accidentally" read it,
and told him how good it was. This direct correlation between having
someone young writers care about value and encourage their writing and
coming to value their writing themselves seems hugely important to me
as an indicator of what makes young people believe in their own talent
and potential.

"FOLLOW THE LEADER": HOW YOUNG RAPPERS
LEARN THE TRICKS OF THE TRADE

A kind of learning that we haven't touched on yet in this chapter is the
kind that grows out of observation, and sometimes concentrated study, of

public models—not those of experienced friends and family, but those available in the popular media. When young people write within Discourses where many public models are available, much of what they understand about the norms of verbal composition in that Discourse comes from observing those whose work they admire. This is where I would argue that those who write song lyrics have an advantage over those who write poetry, in the sense that models of song lyrics of all genres and levels of craft are ubiquitous. An aspiring lyricist has only to decide which genres, styles, and artists they want to listen to and learn from.

In Chapter Four, we examined and challenged the notion of poetry as a purely private genre, and saw examples of the ways that some of The Writers worked with others in the composing, revising, and publication of their poems. However, the poets among The Writers have not thought much about writing as a public Discourse in which they participate with many others and which has certain norms and traditions to which they respond—consciously or not—as they craft their own pieces. The rappers, on the other hand, speak often of what hip-hop as a culture means to them, of the styles of various popular artists working in their Discourse, of the stylistic norms that shape the way that they write. In the most basic terms, then, it seems to me that the poets among The Writers know far less about poetry as a form and as a Discourse than the rappers do about rap and the hip-hop culture of which it is an integral part. The poets don't necessarily think about their writing less, but they think about it in a more individual, even idiosyncratic, way. They have a sense of their own style—their tendency to rhyme or not, their preference for certain subject matter—and they are in some cases able to cite a few famous poets whose work they like. They do not, however, see themselves as being part of a community of poets, and they do not think about their own writing as following from, or responding to, or reflecting specific historical or cultural movements within poetry. In fact, I would argue that even as they call what they write poetry, the stuff that they encounter in their literature textbooks remains relatively alien and inaccessible to them unless they have a teacher who helps them to make connections.

Therefore, to talk about learning from public models among The Writers is to focus on the rappers. Jig, TeTe, Mekanismn, and Crazy admire the wordcraft of specific artists: Nas, DMX, Tupac, and Eminem are among those they regularly cite. Even apparently individual facets of composition, such as the development of a personal style, are learned from attending to the differences among specific artists and regions. Young rappers think about these issues on their own, talk about them with friends, and share them with fellow composers using the apprenticeship and collaboration models discussed at the beginning of this chapter.

Style of delivery is obviously of central importance in rap, whether in freestyle or more extensively crafted lyrics. Jig explains that in freestyle, flexibility is key. Performers know that it is possible that they may get stuck in the middle of a flow; if they do not already have strategies in mind for dealing with this, the flow stops, and the performer loses. Similarly, freestylers aren't always in control of the beat over which they will be flowing; they need strategies for this as well. Jig and TeTe, joined by TeTe's friend Stella, explain:

Jig: If you wind up having a pause or something, you can incorporate that into the next few lines and make them actually go with it and stuff.

TeTe: You can have a real slow beat, and you can rap real fast, like Twista [a popular Chicago rapper known for the speed of his delivery] do, or you can like make the beat fit you. Or you can go with the beat. Either one, it's just like telling a story, only in a rhythm. It's like, "This is a story about this and that," but put it to a rhythm. Like old school, how they used to put it to a rhythm.

SW: What do you mean?

TeTe: Like, what's his name? He used to go "This is a story about . . ."

Stella: Oh—

Stella and Jig: Slick Rick.

TeTe: Yeah, like he used to tell stories about something-something, and he'll make a whole song about it. He just telling a story, and he'll make the beats fit him, and everybody understands it.

A structural element that the rappers learn from models and pass on to one another is that of organizing their rhymes into musical bars, which Jig explains are paired lines, a group of which make up a verse. Traditionally, a bar or measure is a unit containing the rhythmic structure of a given piece of music. When rappers use the term "bar," they are applying a musical term to a lyrical phenomenon. Thus, the common understanding of a rap "bar" as comprising two lines reflects the fact that the rhymed couplet is the basic unit of the rap lyric:

SW: How does it help you as a writer to know what bars are?

TeTe: 'Cause you can count how long it [the verse] needs to be. So you can count, 'Okay, I did these three bars,' or 'Yeah, I freestyled 16 bars,' and not a lot of people can freestyle 16 bars.

Jig: And another thing about it is, if you know what the bars
        are, you can form your thoughts better along with the
        song, you can follow the beat. It'll be better than if you
        just saying it, 'cause then people start getting off beats and
        trying to catch up with the beat. But when you actually
        know what the bars are to the song, then you can form
        your thoughts better along with the song.

If bars are useful in freestyling because they give rappers a mental structure within which to fit their improvisational words, they perform a
slightly different function with written rap lyrics. Writing a rap as a series
of bars, with slashes indicating where lines are separated, creates a sort of
visual map of the rhyme's rhythm, as TeTe explains:

When you just write something, but you don't remember how
you said it when you look back, in a couple of months, you [can]
look back, like, "Okay, I can stop right there, and I can slur it
there."

Jig explains that the structure provided by bars allows a rapper to play
around with a rhyme's delivery without getting lost:

Sometimes with poems and stuff like that, if you want to make
more impact, more influence and something, like, 'My future's
my past/I think it's a bore,' you can start speeding up a little bit
more . . . because there's a set beat and a pattern that it will
follow, constantly.

If oral performance is one key element of rap style, figurative language is clearly another. Metaphor is central to imaginative writing of all
kinds, but perhaps particularly to poetic forms. While young people may
learn the terminology of metaphor in school, they often learn the concept
through popular music and then incorporate it into their own writing.
Crazy describes a favorite metaphor:

One song I did, I was kind of proud, I confused [Jig]. I was like "I
confused my brother, I finally confused him!" He's like, "What
do you mean by that?" It was [about] slavery. 'Cause I seen the
whole thing with a paintbrush, and pen and ink. Normally
people use ink like bullets; they'll say they're firing ink and stuff.
But this time I used it like slavery. Like bullets flying through

fields and everything . . . The paper was the white field, and the black bullets were coming from the pencil, and I was shooting like, I'm shooting it, through your mind, like, I'm sending my knowledge to you.

Jig talks about the way that rapper DMX's lyrics pushed him to think about how writers can play around with references and allusions. He says that the more he listened to DMX's songs, the more he realized that many of the songs are updating biblical stories, modernizing them, replacing, say, a slingshot with a gun: "Like at first I didn't get it, and then I took a bible class in high school, and then in college. I was like 'Oh, I just heard this,' so then I'd go back and listen to it."

Finally, TeTe emphasizes the importance of onomatopoia in verbal performance: "Like, make your tongue go, 'hhhssshhlllppp.' Everybody be like [laughs]. 'Cause if you just say 'slurp' it won't have the same effect."

ACADEMIC AND OUTSIDE LITERACIES: DO THE TWAIN MEET?

> The street is where young bloods get their education. I learned how to talk in the street, not from reading about Dick and Jane going to the zoo and all that simple shit. The teacher would test our vocabulary each week, but we knew the vocabulary we needed. They'd give us arithmetic to exercise our minds. Hell, we exercised our minds by playing the dozens.
> —H. Rap Brown (qtd. in Toop, 2000, 118)

While there are a growing number of studies about both in-school and out-of-school adolescent literacy practices, "we know little about . . . how they weave their unsanctioned or alternative literacies together with academic literacies" (Moje, 2000, p. 653). The subtle ways in which such weaving would occur, and that would make identification and description difficult, may explain the dearth of such studies. Another explanation may lie in researchers' (I include myself here) hesitance to connect "alternative" literacies to school reading and writing too overtly:

> If "you gotta be bad" can be enacted through one's choice in music that advocates sexual and physical violence, for example, then what happens when that avenue becomes sanctioned by

authorities within the school context? The key is to tap into these resources without co-opting them. (Finders, 2002, 102)

Finders' point is important, for if youth enact certain kinds of resistance through reading and writing, then to co-opt such enactments is to take from students a valuable tool, and to cause them, perhaps, to reach out for new ways to prove their resistance—ways that may be less productive than an engagement with verbal texts.

However, the lack of documentation of how out-of-school and class-room literacy practices work together may also stem from the fact that they work together in limited ways. If true, this would help to explain the dilemma of young people who are prolific writers of rap and poetry but are not particularly adept at standardized usage or "essayist" (Collins and Blot, 2003, 44) literacies. The Writers had little difficulty identifying the gaps between what they more often than not see as two distinct worlds. Jig says,

> I think you learn more, actually, from this creative style of writing, than what you do in school, 'cause they telling you what to do. It have to be this way, that way, so you can write in one teacher's style, and then you go to the next class, and they say, "No, you don't do it like that." So it's totally different.

SW: So with this stuff you can develop your own style.
Jig: Right, in school I just adapt it to the teacher.

Mekanismn concurs:

> When I write for myself, it's stuff that I'm going through, or stuff that I see, or stuff that's funny. But stuff that I write for school is school purpose.

SW: You seem pretty confident about yourself as a music writer. Do you have that same confidence in your-self as a writer of papers?
Mekanismn: Yes and no. Well, yeah, yeah—I'd say yeah.
SW: And does it . . .
Mekanismn: 'Cause I know how to write.
SW: So it translates in the way you put ideas together.
Mekanismn: Yeah.
SW: So you actually enjoy writing stuff . . .
Mekanismn: I love writing. Not for school, but . . . It's cool, though, you know, I'm more just for my purpose is

> writing lyrics, writing for hip hop. It's nothing,
> though, to write for school, it's like whatever, type it
> up, whatever, same thing, really.

Mekanismn's reflexive corrections to his initial responses about school literacy ("Yes and no. Well, yeah, yeah—I'd say yeah" and "I love writing. Not for school, but . . . It's cool, though") suggest that he thinks there are things he *should* believe about the connections between in-school and out-of-school writing, such as that his ability to write rap lyrics means that he can just as easily write academic essays. Obviously, I cannot say for sure what motivates this move on Mekanismn's part, but I can't help thinking of Christensen's "language of power," and of the public criticisms of "Ebonics" and of hip-hop discussed in the second and third chapters of this book. A desire to defend the writing that he loves, by suggesting that it *does* translate into quality school writing, and that it is on the same level as other kinds of writing, is understandable. Yet I wonder if the desire to protect the Discourses they favor might actually work against writers like Mekanismn, motivating them to deny difficulties they may have in some genres of writing for fear that these less-developed skills will reflect badly on the forms of writing they do regularly. This may be one of the many kinds of damage done by the mainstream devaluing of Discourses that are connected in the popular imagination to a specific ethnoracial group, to a specific generation, or to perceived deviancy. By forcing those who work within these Discourses into a defensive stance, critics make it much less likely that candid conversations or productive cross-pollination will occur.

There are positive stories as well, though. A number of the writers spoke of specific classrooms in which they were able to draw on their skills and experience. TeTe's friend Stella tells of having "poetry battles" in her English class, and Jig recalls a creative writing course in which "every day inside the class, you have to put everything away, take out one piece of paper and a pencil, and the teacher wrote one word on the board, and we'd have like one or two minutes in order to write a story or a poem or something to it." For youth who are motivated by challenge, competition with peers, and flexibility in their approach to a piece of writing, activities like these stood out as positive classroom experiences.

There were also stories of connecting with canonical texts in school. Stella, a writer of poetry, described one such text:

> There was a book. I don't remember the thing, [something like] 'I heard a fly . . .'

SW: "I heard a fly buzz when I died"? That's Emily Dickinson.

Stella: Yeah, that's kind of deep, and it scared me, and got me to think, like, "Maaan." I don't know how the poem goes, but it's good. She was the type, all she wrote about was death.

TeTe: Oh, she like Jig.

These writers can sometimes see themselves, and one another, in canonical authors much as they can in popular rappers or in the poetry of peers in the school literary magazine. I recall reading a piece of writing by a female student when I first started working at *La Juventud*. A particular turn of phrase—lost to me now—struck me then, and I told her that it reminded me of Shakespeare's style. For the next several days, she made a point of informing other teachers that Susan had called her writing "Shakespearean."

I also recall when another *LJ* student, Michelle, approached me in the library during lunch and handed me a piece of notebook paper with three poems on it—she wanted me to consider them for the upcoming literary magazine. I read the first one, "Beauty":

Beautiful Roses, or beautiful
anything will make you smile.
But beauty could only last
a little while.

The rose will wilt and die.

I asked Michelle if she had ever read S.E. Hinton's *The Outsiders* (1997 [1967]), because her poem sounded like the one by Robert Frost that is featured in that novel. Michelle said no, though her friends had told her it was good. We walked over to the fiction shelf and searched until we found it. I opened the book, flipping the pages to Frost's poem, "Nothing Gold Can Stay." After Michelle read it, I asked her if she saw any similarities to her poem. Michelle said yes, and we discussed how both poems seemed to be about beautiful things going away or fading. Michelle decided to check the book out (Weinstein, 2002, 39).

It may be that the most productive connections that educators can, at least initially, make between out-of-school and in-school literacies have less to do with specific lesson designs than with demonstrating respect for, interest in, and (hopefully) a growing understanding of young people's own worlds and words. "There do not have to be inherent discontinuities between young people's authentic life experiences and their experience of life in schools," Mahiri writes, yet some of the very *perspectives* and *technologies* that facilitate the sourcing of multitextual, multimodal, multicultural resources for learning are the ones least used or developed, especially in urban schools. (2004, 14, italics added)

In order to advocate for such resources, educators first have to develop an understanding of youths' out-of-school practices, which for some adults will require substantial shifts in their ways of thinking about popular culture, correctness, and literary validity. Even then, of course, not all schools will have the same access to the more advanced technologies to which Mahiri refers above. Every person reading this, though, can alter their *perspectives* on youths' experiences and abilities. I read it as no accident that Mahiri puts "perspectives" ahead of "technologies" in identifying what schools need to develop, and it is my sincere hope that this chapter—and this book—will contribute to just such changes in perspective among educators and other youth workers.

CONCLUSION

This chapter is not meant as a defense of young people's imaginative writing. One could—and some scholars do—employ similar data as part of a strategy for legitimizing devalued Discourses by arguing that they are, in fact, *just like* mainstream Discourses, or that they can serve as *bridges* to engagement with mainstream Discourses, or that they are interesting *additions* to mainstream Discourses. There is certainly good reason to make this gesture:

> An acceptance of . . . essayist literacy as normative condemns those whose ways of making meaning and of taking meaning from text vary from the norm to a perpetual struggle to legitimate their own practices. (Collins & Blot, 2003, p. 44)

Such gestures of legitimation, though, reinforce the ingrained normativity of standardized practices. It's a fine line to walk, because it's a hard line to actually see—where does a detailed description of an alternative practice become a defense of said practice? This is, however, exactly the line I have tried to negotiate in this book. Yet I recognize that in a hierarchical system, it may be impossible to foreground a devalued form without the specter of more highly valued forms always in the background as the unarticulated unit of comparison. I suspect that I have been unsuccessful in fully avoiding the assimilationist gestures I mention above. It is out of a consciousness of the problematic nature of such gestures, however, that there are no specific recommendations in this book about how teachers can use the concepts here in classroom lessons. If I cannot avoid having legitimation be one of the conscious or inadvertent outcomes of this book, I can at least keep the focus on description and analysis of The Writers' literacies and not repeatedly emphasize the need to bring it all back to the strengthening of students' skills in standardized language and literacies.

One thing I *have* tried to illustrate is that there is shared ground among a variety of literacy-based Discourses. The Writers often go through several drafts of a piece of writing. They value good, critical feedback—as long as they trust the person giving the feedback. They want to know how others read their work, and they get pleasure from thoughtful responses. They enjoy playing around with words, style, and form, and they think about the sensory experiences ("hhhssshhlllppp") that both they and their audiences get from a piece.

The Writers—and others like them—are engaged in exciting intellectual work. This work is often either denigrated or unrecognized because of its crafters' social positioning and/or because of the genres they favor. The Writers know this. And they keep writing, because the experience of being one who writes (as any committed writer in any genre knows) is powerful and satisfying in ways that those who dismiss or ignore youths' imaginative writing don't even try to understand.

8

"If You Can't Write You Can't Succeed"

CHANGING ATTITUDES AMONG EDUCATORS AND YOUTH

You know the kid's gonna act a fool
When you stop the programs for after school
And they DCFS,[1] some of them dyslexic
They favorite 50 Cent song's "12 Questions"[2]
We scream, "Rock, blow, weed, park"
See now we smart
We ain't retards the way teachers thought
Hold up hold fast we make more cash
Now tell my momma I belong in the slow class . . .

(West, 2004b)

— —

Linda: "I can't write"

Linda says, "Writing is really important. If you can't write, you can't succeed. You have to have it to succeed in life." It's clear that she's really taken this common wisdom to heart, and so she has pretty much decided that she can't succeed because she can't write.

Then she says, "Well, look at you, Susan. You're smart, and you're working on your doctorate in college and everything, and you're working here. Why would you be working here? And if you have all that education and you can write really well, and you're still working here, what am *I* gonna have to do to be able to get a good job?"

Linda: "I have a lot to say"

After class, tutoring Linda one-on-one in the empty student lounge, I ask her what she wants to write about. She says she only has four classes; the only one that has writing is her Life Skills class, and that's journaling, which she doesn't want to do. I say, "Let's work on the literacy history," an assignment she has for my creative writing class. I tell her to pick one of the introductory paragraphs she has already worked on, and then to keep writing while I step out for a few minutes. Before I leave, I talk about prewriting, mentioning that some people make lists, although I like to outline. I sketch a small concept web and explain how that works. I tell her that some people find it helpful to see their ideas laid out like that, though I don't use them myself. She says, "Me either." Then she adds, "I just want to be able to sit down and write an essay from my head," meaning, I take it, that that's how she thinks good writers do it.

She asks what the literacy history is supposed to be about. I explain, at which point she says, "I already wrote that," which it turns out that she has, for another teacher who regularly uses this assignment. Linda says, "I could still write it."

I say, "But it wouldn't be very interesting to you."

"It would be easy, though, since I already wrote it all."

I tap my knuckles on the wooden table for emphasis as I say, "Ah, but this has nothing to do with easy." I suggest she write about why she hates school so much, since we have been talking about that for the last half hour. As she picks up her pen, she says,

"So write about how I hate school?"

"And why," I add.

"I have a lot to say for that."

"I know."

— —

Linda is not one of the writers in this study. She was a student at *La Juventud* who had come out of a K-8 bilingual public school program. Seventeen at the time of the above conversations, she had a long history of struggle with reading and writing. She qualified for special education services, which at *LJ* meant that she would meet for one hour a week with a school board-appointed special education instructor who covered several schools around the city. Sometimes, though, those services were not available. And sometimes she would miss her meetings because she had a habit of skipping school.

I include Linda's story here, despite the well-known—and well-founded—rule that says one should never introduce a new character this late in a narrative. Linda represents, in terms of literacy, the flip side of the nine writers in this study. Like them, she was hungry to develop her intelligence. Like them, as she says in the second vignette above, she had "a lot to say." Unlike them, however, the basic skills that would have enabled Linda to expand her knowledge through reading, and to say what she had to say through writing, remained elusive to her. There is no one person or institution to blame for this—as we have seen throughout this book, literacy is deeply intertwined with one's family and community backgrounds, with one's experiences in school and on the streets, with one's physical strengths and weaknesses as well as one's psychic pleasure and pain.

Having said that, I can't help but feel that Linda's ways of thinking about writing, as illustrated in her words, are representative of many, many young people's. The first vignette demonstrates that she had clearly internalized the ideology that equates literacy with professional success and financial stability. Instead of being motivated by this equation, however, Linda felt doomed by it. Having experienced more failure than success with reading and writing, the equation for her became reframed in negative terms: the lack of literacy skills equals the lack of a stable future. She could see tiny chinks in this ideology, as evidenced by her puzzlement that I, a highly educated person—an English teacher no less—was "stuck" working at *La Juventud*, a workplace she didn't find impressive at all (when I explained that I wasn't even getting paid to be there, she became even more confused). The only conclusion she seemed able to draw was that it must take even more literacy skills than I had to get anywhere really interesting, which made it seem less conceivable than ever that she would get anywhere at all. The attitudes that Linda reflects toward literacy, the things she believes, are very much in keeping with the way literacy instruction is delivered in school. For Linda, the results of these attitudes are frustration with her present and doubt about her future, an inaccurate understanding of how people "do" writing when they have a reason to do it, and a sense that there is no reason to write other than because someone says you have to.

At the beginning of Chapter Seven, I quoted an article by Linda Christensen. In that article, Christensen writes of the tension between advocating a pedagogy that emphasizes attention to young people's experiences, desires, and needs and knowing that failing to learn standardized English skills handcuffs students. Like Lisa Delpit (1995) before her, Christensen voices a caution to progressive educators that I have always found important and necessary. Yet, there is a danger that in our mission to help marginalized youth gain access to cultural capital, we will simply end up reinforcing the views of writing that made Linda feel so hopeless, since such views

> promote a stance that all we need to do to remove inequity and improve our material and social conditions is learn how to write well. But what does writing 'well' mean? Who gets to decide? Could everyone actually be viewed as writing well? If everyone did write well, would inequity disappear? Would we all have access to power? (Sheridan et al., 212)

Reading over the preceding chapters, similar questions occur to me, related not only to writing but to forms of language: *what if more kinds of language shared power? What if individuals speaking African American Vernacular English or Spanglish, people talking in the accents of Philadelphia's Main Line and of the Appalachian back country could somehow learn to listen to each other—not to ignore the accents and diverse dialects, but to recognize them as an integral part of the conversation? What if, in other words, everyone had an equal voice in the spheres of power, for the basic reasons that they are all part of this society and their experiences in some way impact everyone else's?*

These are hard thoughts for me to admit to—I realize how idealistic they sound. But it is *so easy* to fall into believing that the only job in town, education-wise, is to help young people fit into the structure-as-it-is. This is, after all, the function of ideology—to make *one* option seem like the *only* option. In the case of languages and literacies, the ideology is regularly reinforced because—in the short-term, for individual students—fitting into that structure *is* important. One's ability to earn money, to pursue goals, to raise families—all of these things are connected to (though not completely determined by) one's ability to talk certain kinds of talk and walk certain kinds of walk.

However, the first, small step in altering an ingrained ideology is to imagine alternatives. And imagining alternatives requires at least a smidgen of idealism, if idealism means having an image in one's head and heart of how one wishes things could be. Whether the ideal can be reached . . . well, power and money are inextricably linked in a capitalist society, and to believe that people in different socioeconomic situations are going to run to each other open-armed as the scales of linguistic prejudice fall from their eyes (ears?), just because someone has explained the problems, goes beyond idealism into a useless naivete.

So what do we do? How do we address "the problem of 'Monday morning'" (Willis, 1977, 186)—that is, the concrete needs of specific individuals *right now*—while simultaneously working toward our ideals?

And how do we justify our ideals while recognizing that our reach will always exceed our grasp? Willis writes,

> there is no contradiction in asking practitioners to work on two levels simultaneously—to face immediate problems in doing "the best" (so far as they can see it) for their clients whilst appreciating all the time that these very actions may help to reproduce the structures within which the problems arise . . . To contract out of the messy business of day to day problems is to deny the active, contested nature of social and cultural reproduction: to condemn real people to the status of passive zombies, and actually cancel the future by default. (1977, 186)

We must respect the young people we work with. We must develop curricula and programs that challenge all youth, while drawing on their existing interests and abilities. We must consciously seek to learn about those interests and abilities. We must preach to the choir, and then visit other denominations. We must help disseminate the ideas of people whose voices are not traditionally heard. We must become involved in political action, organizing around one, some, or many of the societal issues that affect young people's material conditions—issues of housing, of racial discrimination, of educational inequity, and of access to health care, to name a few. We must share our firsthand knowledge of the power that literacy has for young people of all classes and ethnoracial descriptions when it is experienced alongside support, caring, honesty, and commitment.

What I have learned more than anything else from this research is how complex youths' imaginative writing is. The teenage years are full of confusion and contradiction as young people try on different roles, test the values they have received as children, and constantly try to grasp that elusive "self" that they claim so insistently even as they are changing and growing. For some youth, like the nine in this book, imaginative writing is a central way of giving full play to this complicated stage of development. It is no surprise, therefore, that many of The Writers see little or no connection between the writing they are required to do in school and that which they spend so much time and energy on outside of the classroom. Academic writing generally requires clarity, linear organization, a well-defined point-of-view, and a decisive conclusion. The Writers require imaginative space to play, to try on ideas without committing to them or being held to them by others, to say what they're not supposed to say just to see what it feels like to be "that" person. There is room in a young person's mind, I believe, for both kinds of writing; in fact, there doesn't have to be a clear separation between them. To find ways to make connections, however, educators need to understand the dynamics underlying and motivating each kind of composition. It is my hope that this book will provide educators and others with just such an understanding.

Epilogue: Where Are They Now?

The only thing that you're ever promised in this world . . . is the words that you speak. No matter how you speak it, that is all you have and there is no one . . . that can ever take that away from you.

—Crazy

Author's Note: I originally wrote the entries in this Epilogue in the spring of 2004. Since then, I've kept in fairly consistent contact with a few of The Writers. Unfortunately, the nature of low-income urban existence is such that I've lost contact with several of The Writers—phones are shut off, living arrangements change with some regularity . . . As a result, some of the updates below are more up-to-date than others. The Writers whose names are in bold below wrote their own updates in fall/winter 2007. I wrote the remaining entries in 2004.

A. *Crazy* writes, "I'm not in school anymore at the moment but I plan on going to get my license in business. I have been working two jobs. One is being an assistant teacher teaching Digital Photography and Graphic Design with [the former graphic arts teacher at *La Juventud*] at a high school. The other is teaching life skills and training through team building at a university. However, I am now currently working on getting a Real Estate business going with my father, temporarily though, just until I have enough money to invest inside of my own music and t-shirt equipment. After that I'm going full time into making music, producing tracks, and creating my own clothing line pretty much.

Um, as far as my writing goes . . . me getting inspired now is kind of difficult only because there's really nothing out there as far as real artistry. I mean there's nothing that plays on the radio now except for pretty much garbage songs . . . yea it'll be good for the club but, to only play that on the radio and nothing from artists like Joe Budden, Ghostface, Nas, Jadakiss, Beanie Sigel, Collie Buddz, Method Man, Redman, Talib Kweli, Mos Def, Lupe Fiasco and there's plenty more.

161

I'm thinking about changing my artist name again to Lyrical the Phantom of Life . . . so far I have Lyrical the Sage of an Emcee, Lyrical the Oasis of a Poet (those are the two that I currently go by) but I may just stick with Lyrical the Phantom of Life. Oh yea, I have a connect at this underground lounge and the owner said I can come in any time I want and do a show, so hopefully I can get my stuff together soon cause people is still waiting to hear things and after it's heard I know they will buy."

B. *Dave* writes, "I am currently living in Miami with no immediate plans of returning to Chicago. While I miss the culture in Chicago, I accept the fact that 'you can't go home again.' Things change and so must I. Adaptation. I am currently studying in a Miami college with plans to transfer to another university to become a professor of psychology and a basketball coach. I am currently working at a school coaching basketball and working in their after school program. I am still estranged from my father with whom I have had a difficult past. I write when the inspiration comes to me. I draw more frequently now as well as reading books from comic book graphic novels to Genghis Khan and philosophy. I feel I have a better handle on my life. Holding life by the neck sort of viewpoint."

C. *Jig* writes, "Jig Insane is currently re-writing his entire catalogue of lyrics due to his older lyrics being erased by a computer virus. He currently resides on Chicago's West-Side and is the supervisor of catering and cafeteria services for [the food service company at the community college he attended]. He also works part-time for the Conservatory Alliance helping to educate the community about the wonders of nature."

D. *José*—Driving to my apartment in the Pilsen neighborhood of Chicago in early April 2004, I did a double-take as I saw a young man crossing the street in front of my car and realized it was José, whom I had tried to contact a couple of times in the past months without success. I pulled my car over and called to him, and we chatted for a few minutes. He told me that he has worked out his immigration problems, and is now a legal resident of the United States. That afternoon, he was on his way to the local library to pick up an application for Job Corps, a program that trains youth for work in a variety of fields.

E. *Marta*—Last time I spoke with Marta, she told me that she was planning to move in with her current boyfriend, who owns a house in a suburb of Chicago. She gave me three different contact numbers; at the moment, however, two of them don't seem to belong to her anymore, and the other has no answering machine. I am continuing to try to reach her.

F. *Mekanismn* writes, "As of lately I been working hard. I'm still doing the music thing. I been writing like crazy. I have at least 25 songs that I planned on recording and putting them on a mixtape. But I'm just keeping my focus until the opportunity presents itself for me to get a deal. And even if it never does I'm still going to write. But I take any opportunity that presents itself."

G. *Patricia* gave birth to her third child on March 31, 2004. When last we spoke, she was working at home to complete the courses she needed to graduate from *La Juventud*. She is planning to move to a larger apartment on Chicago's West Side soon. With school, occasional part-time work, and now three small children, she does not have much time to write.

H. *Robbie* got kicked out of *La Juventud* in November 2003, many credits shy of graduation. He had already been expelled a number of times for truancy, marijuana use during school hours, and/or disrespect to teachers and administrators. This time they said that he couldn't come back. Since then, he's been working on his music, writing lyrics, and playing guitar. He said he's put some of the poems he shared with me to music. He has started a band with a friend, and describes their sound as "Pink Floyd meets Ministry." When I spoke to him on the phone in late April 2004, he told me that he had gotten tickets to see the Canadian band Rush in concert in June—I couldn't help waxing nostalgic about listening to Rush when I was in high school, and he was very patient with me. He has no immediate plans to return to high school or work toward a GED; "I'm really putting all of my time into my music right now," he says.

I. *TeTe* now goes by the name Reality. She writes, "These days I am studying to be a medical assistant. After that I'm going for my RN—gotta have a backup plan. And I have a 2yr old daughter now so I had to get a little mature but I haven't given up on my dream. I still write and I do catch myself listening to people spit [lyrics] and getting excited to do it again but I see myself more into directing the videos instead of starring in them, writing and directing the movies, maybe doing some acting too, but I wouldn't want to act in my own, writing a couple fictional novels. So be lookin' out for me but I still wouldn't mind spitting on the side only as long as my brothers are by my side while I'm doing it :)".

—-—

Appendix

AMENDED [Jan. 15, 1997]
RESOLUTION OF THE
BOARD OF EDUCATION
ADOPTING THE REPORT AND RECOMMENDATIONS
OF THE AFRICAN-AMERICAN TASK FORCE;
A POLICY STATEMENT
AND
DIRECTING THE SUPERINTENDENT OF SCHOOLS
TO DEVISE A PROGRAM TO IMPROVE THE
ENGLISH LANGUAGE ACQUISITION AND APPLICATION
SKILLS
OF AFRICAN-AMERICAN STUDENTS
No. 9697–0063

WHEREAS, numerous validated scholarly studies demonstrate that African-American students as a part of their culture and history as African people possess and utilize a language described in various scholarly approaches as "Ebonics" (literally "Black sounds") or "Pan African Communication Behaviors" or "African Language Systems"; and

WHEREAS, these studies have also demonstrated that African Language Systems have origins in West and Niger-Congo languages and are not merely dialects of English; and

WHEREAS, these studies demonstrate that such West and Niger-Congo African languages have been recognized and addressed in the educational community as worthy of study, understanding and application of their principles, laws and structures for the benefit of African-American students both in terms of positive appreciation of the language and these students' acquisition and mastery of English language skills; and

WHEREAS, such recognition by scholars has given rise over the past fifteen years to legislation passed by the State of California recognizing

165

the unique language stature of descendants of slaves, with such legislation being prejudicially and unconstitutionally vetoed repeatedly by various California state governors; and

WHEREAS, judicial cases in states other than California have recognized the unique language stature of African American pupils, and such recognition by courts has resulted in court-mandated educational programs which have substantially benefited African-American children in the interest of vindicating their equal protection of the law rights under the Fourteenth Amendment to the United States Constitution; and

WHEREAS, the Federal Bilingual Education Act (20 U.S.C. 1402 *et seq.*) mandates that local educational agencies "build their capacities to establish, implement and sustain programs of instruction for children and youth of limited English proficiency; and

WHEREAS, the interest of the Oakland Unified School District in providing equal opportunities for all of its students dictate limited English proficient educational programs recognizing the English language acquisition and improvement skills of African-American students are as fundamental as is application of bilingual or second language learner principles for others whose primary languages are other than English. Primary languages are the language patterns children bring to school; and

WHEREAS, the standardized tests and grade scores of African-American students in reading and language arts skills measuring their application of English skills are substantially below state and national norms and that such deficiencies will be remedied by application of a program featuring African Language Systems principles to move students from the language patterns they bring to school to English proficiency; and

WHEREAS, standardized tests and grade scores will be remedied by application of a program that teachers and instructional assistants, who are certified in the methodology of African Language Systems principles used to transition students from the language patterns they bring to school to English. The certified teachers of these students will be provided incentives including, but not limited to Leoary differentials;

NOW, THEREFORE, BE IT RESOLVED that the Board of Education officially recognizes the existence, and the cultural and historic bases of West and Niger-Congo African Language Systems, and each language as the primary language of many African-American students; and

BE IT FURTHER RESOLVED that the Board of Education hereby adopts the report, recommendations and attached Policy Statement of the District's African-American Task Force on the language stature of African-American speech; and

BE IT FURTHER RESOLVED that the Superintendent in conjunction with her staff shall immediately devise and implement the best possible academic program for the combined purposes of facilitating the acquisition and mastery of English language skills, while respecting and embracing the legitimacy and richness of the language patterns whether they are known as "Ebonics," "African Language Systems," "Pan African Communication Behaviors," or other description; and

BE IT FURTHER RESOLVED that the Board of Education hereby commits to earmark District general and special funding as is reasonably necessary and appropriate to enable the Superintendent and her staff to accomplish the foregoing; and

BE IT FURTHER RESOLVED that the Superintendent and her staff shall utilize the input of the entire Oakland educational community as well as state and federal scholarly and educational input in devising such a program; and

BE IT FURTHER RESOLVED that periodic reports on the progress of the creation and implementation of such an educational program shall be made to the Board of Education at least once per month commencing at the Board meeting of December 18, 1996.

Notes

INTRODUCTION

1. Throughout this book, I will refer to these young women and men collectively as The Writers, in order to avoid repeating ad nauseum "the writers in this study" and to clarify when I am referring specifically to these nine and not to writers generally or to some other group of writers.
2. "Patricia," "Marta," "José," "Robbie," and "Dave" are pseudonyms. For the four rappers in the group—Jig, Mekanismn, Crazy, and TéTé—I have used the actual rap names they were using at the time of this research, as well as the actual name of their group, The Maniacs. This is per their request.
3. Throughout this book, I will return to Gee's concept of capital "D" Discourse and will signal this by using the capital D.
4. Literally, "latin-ness," or the experience of being Hispanic/Latino.

CHAPTER ONE: "I AM ME BUT WHO AM I?"

1. Crazy, his brother Jig, and his sister TéTé all post writing on a message board thread on the website of R&B singer Alicia Keys. Like many contemporary youth, these three are fans of both rap and rhythm and blues; Alicia Keys has been a guest artist on a number of rap records, which adds to her crossover appeal.
2. I worked as an assistant director at the University of Illinois at Chicago Writing Center for two years during my PhD program.
3. A socially conscious Chicago hip-hopper who moved to New York City.
4. "Chi" as in "Chi-town," as in Chicago.

5. dead prez are a political, Afro-centric hip-hop group; *Let's Get Free* is the title of one of the group's CDs.

CHAPTER TWO: "YOU NEVER LET ME SPEAK"

1. Accessed on 7/26/03 at http://papyr.com/ hypertextbooks/ engl_126/ ateg.htm.

CHAPTER THREE: "QUESTIONING MYSELF AND THE PEOPLE AROUND ME"

1. See Dwight McBride (2002) for an extended discussion of the authority of personal experience claimed by the authors of slave narratives and by their abolitionist supporters.

CHAPTER FOUR: "YOU GOTTA BE A WRITER TO GET IN THE GAME"

1. Interview excerpt aired on "MTV2 Presents 22 Greatest MC's" air date July 6, 2003.
2. Track—a rap recorded on an audio tape or compact disc.
3. See Mos Def, "Close Edge" (2004): "I'm the catalog/You the same song."
4. In other words, keeping their battles confined to tapes or CDs ("wax" of course being a reference to the now-almost-completely-outmoded LP record), rather than letting them lead to physical confrontations.
5. Jacob and Company, an exclusive jeweler popular with (and regularly referenced in song by) successful rappers.
6. It's ironic that the principal uses the 50 Cent cover image as a symbol of rap's qualitative decline, since widely respected lyricist KRS ONE's late-'80s album *Criminal Minded* (with Boogie Down Productions) features a similar image.
7. *Hip hop and social change conference* keynote speech, Field Museum, Chicago, IL, October 4, 2003.
8. The terms *shine* and *floss* here both mean to show off through public displays of material wealth.
9. Referencing the Reconstruction promise to ex-slaves of "forty acres and a mule."

10. As an interesting side note, the word *pimp* was the subject of a lawsuit after the cable sports channel ESPN posted a photograph of daredevil Evel Knievel, his wife, and another woman on one of its websites with the caption, "Evel Knievel proves you're never too old to be a pimp." Knievel sued the channel for libel, but the Ninth Circuit Court of Appeals ruled that "We think that any reasonable viewer would have interpreted the word 'pimp' in the loose, figurative sense . . .", and that its current slang connotation was positive, meaning something akin to the word *cool* (accessed at http://www.gannett.com/go/newswatch/2005/january/nw0114-3.htm on 22 Dec. 2007).

11. In the film *8 Mile*, Eminem's character Rabbit is loving and protective toward his younger sister, who appears to be about 6 years old.

CHAPTER FIVE: PREGNANCY, PIMPS & "CLICHÉD LOVE THINGS"

1. Note to readers: this chapter includes sexually graphic poetry and rap lyrics.

2. A song from the 2002 CD *The Eminem Show*: "How could it ever be just us two, I'd never love you enough to trust you/we just met and I just fucked you . . ."

3. Recently, I played the video for this song, which I had downloaded onto my laptop, for a former student, Lori. We watched it together, then sat silently for a second before Lori—who already knew the song well—whispered, "Man, that's *too* deep."

CHAPTER SIX: "MY WORK SPARKED AN INTEREST IN SOMEONE ELSE"

1. The process of developing a conscious and critical understanding of one's social positioning through reading and writing.

2. The "pioneering radio show 'Mr. Magic's Rap Attack' aired Fridays and Saturdays . . . on WBLS, a black-owned New York station better known for its R&B predilections than for its hip hop sensibilities" (Light, 1999, 103). Mr. Magic was the host; Marley Marl was the show's engineer/DJ.

3. Mos Def's entire album *Black on Both Sides*, in fact, is a study in intertextuality.

4. Eminem's 2003 movie *8 Mile* offers several examples of this kind of formalized battle.
5. Knobel (1999) offers an example of the effect of discouraging pleasure in school activities. She writes of a 7th grade student, Hannah, who is quiet and self-effacing in the classroom, but who often develops and acts out skits with her girlfriends during lunch, skits which her classroom teacher often allows the girls to perform in front of the class. When Hannah participated in a practice session with the school's drama group, she initially incorporated the same exuberance, play, and risk-taking that was evident in the lunch-time play-acting. However,

> one of the two teachers present interrupted Hannah's performance to tell her to 'speak in your normal, clear voice,' and the other teacher told Hannah she was speaking too quickly. For a fleeting moment Hannah looked crestfallen, then she took a deep breath and began again. This time, she more or less talked the part through, and her gestures and movements were much more restrained, even wooden. (170)

CHAPTER SEVEN: "I'M BOOK SMART, STREET SMART & EVERYTHING IN BETWEEN"

1. Cipher: a circle in which rappers trade improvisational lines.
2. A similar example comes from rapper Rakim in the song "Follow the Leader": "Pull out my weapon and start to squeeze/A magnum as a microphone murderin' MC's" (Griffin Jr., 1988).

CHAPTER EIGHT: IF YOU CAN'T WRITE YOU CAN'T SUCCEED

1. DCFS: Department of Children and Family Services.
2. A play on "21 Questions," a hit song by rapper 50 Cent.

Works Cited

No author. (2001). Access denied: Restoring the nation's commitment to equal educational opportunity. Washington, D.C.: Advisory Committee on Student Financial Assistance.

No author. (2004). Reading the world [Electronic]. *The Council chronicle.* Retrieved September from http://www.ncte.org/pubs/chron/samp/117632.htm.

Allensworth, E., & Rosencranz, T. (2000). Access to magnet high schools in Chicago. Chicago: Consortium for Chicago School Research.

Allensworth, E. (2005). Report highlights. *Graduation and dropout trends in Chicago: A look at cohorts of students from 1991 through 2004.* Chicago: Consortium on Chicago School Research at the University of Chicago.

Althusser, L. (1977). Ideology and ideological state apparatuses (Notes towards an investigation). In *Lenin and philosophy and other essays.* London: New Left Books.

Anzaldua, G. (1987). *Borderlands/la frontera: The new Mestiza.* San Francisco: Aunt Lute Books.

B-boys.com. (2005). Unofficial hip-hop timeline. Retrieved February 13, 2005, from http://www.b-boys.com/hiphoptimeline.html.

Bakhtin, M. (1986). *Speech genres and other late essays.* Austin: University of Texas Press.

Barthes, R. (1975). *The pleasure of the text* (R. Miller, Trans.). New York: Hill and Wang.

Barton, D., Hamilton, M., & Ivanic, R. (Ed.). (2000). *Situated literacies: Reading and writing in context.* London: Routledge.

Baugh, J. (1999). *Out of the mouths of slaves: African American language and educational malpractice.* Austin: University of Texas Press.

Baumann, G. (1999). *The multicultural riddle: Rethinking national, ethnic, and religious identities.* New York: Routledge.

Bettie, J. (2002). *Women without class: Girls, race, and identity*. Berkeley: University of California Press.

Bourdieu, P., & Passeron, J. (1990). *Reproduction in education, society, and culture*. London: Sage.

Bozza, A. (2003). *Whatever you say I am: The life and times of Eminem*. New York: Three Rivers Press.

Brandt, D. (2001). *Literacy in American lives*. Cambridge, UK: Cambridge U.P.

Christensen, L. (2003). The politics of correction [Electronic Version]. *Rethinking schools* online 18: 20–24 from http://www.rethinkingschools.org/archive/18_01/18_01.shtml.

Cisneros, S. (1984). *The house on Mango Street*. New York: Random House.

———. (1992). *My wicked, wicked ways*. New York: Knopf.

Collins, A., & Holum, A. (1991). Cognitive apprenticeship: Making thinking visible [Electronic Version]. *American educator*. Retrieved May 29, 2005 from http://www.21learn.org/arch/articles/brown_seely.html.

Collins, J., & Blot, R. (2003). *Literacy and literacies: Texts, power, and identity*. Cambridge: Cambridge U.P.

Courtney, M. (2004). Best Interests of the Child—Changing Definitions. *"40 Years of Stewardship . . . Where Are We Headed?" A report on the DCFS 40th Anniversary Symposium*. Chicago: Illinois Department of Children and Family Services.

Cross, B. (1993). *It's not about a salary: Rap, race, and resistance in Los Angeles*. New York: W.W. Norton & Co., Inc.

Csikszentmihalyi, M. (1996). *Creativity: Flow and the psychology of discovery and invention*. New York: Harper Collins.

Cushman, E. (1998). *The struggle and the tools: Oral and literate strategies in an inner city community*. Albany: State University of New York Press.

D12. (2001). Purple pills. On *Devil's night* [Audio recording]. Santa Monica: Shady/Interscope Records.

dead prez. (2000). They schools. On *Let's get free* [Audio recording]. Woodland Hills, CA: Loud Records.

de Castell, S., Luke, A., & Egan, K. (Eds.). (1986). *Literacy, society, and schooling: A reader*. Cambridge: Cambridge U.P.

deCerteau, M. (1984). *The practice of everyday life*. Berkeley: University of California Press.

Delpit, L. (1995). *Other people's children: Cultural conflict in the classroom*. New York: The New Press.

Dewey, J. (2001). *The school and society/The child and the curriculum*. Mineola, NY: Dover.

Dickinson, E. (1998). I heard a fly buzz. In R. W. Franklin (Ed.). *The poems of Emily Dickinson*. Cambridge, MA: Belknap Press.

Dorfman, L. & Schiraldi, V. (2001). *Off balance: Youth, race, & crime in the news fact sheet*. Washington, D.C.: Building Blocks for Youth.

Dyson, M. E. (2001). *Holler if you hear me: Searching for Tupac Shakur*. New York: Basic Civitas.

Eve. (1999). Heaven only knows. On *Ruff Ryders' first lady* [Audio recording]. Santa Monica: Interscope Records.

Finders, M. (2002). Literacy, gender, and adolescence: School-sponsored English as identity maintenance. In R. L. Yagelski & S. Leonard (Ed.). *The relevance of English: Teaching that matters in students' lives*. Urbana, IL: NCTE.

Fine, M. (1991). *Framing dropouts: Notes on the politics of an urban public high school*. Albany: State University of New York Press.

Freire, P. (1997). *Pedagogy of the oppressed*. New York: Continuum.

Frick, J., & Ahearn, C. (2002). *Yes yes y'all: The Experience Music Project oral history of hip-hop's first decade*. Cambridge, MA: Da Capo Press.

Gans, H. (1999). *Popular culture and high culture: An analysis and evaluation of taste*. New York: Basic Books.

Gee, J. (1996). *Social linguistics and literacies: Ideology in discourses* (2 ed.). London: Taylor & Francis.

Gilligan, C., & Brown, L. M. (1992). *Meeting at the crossroads: Women's psychology and girls' development*. New York: Ballantine.

Gilyard, K. (1996). *Let's flip the script: An African American discourse on language, literature, and learning*. Detroit: Wayne State Press.

Giroux, H. (1991). *Border crossings: Cultural workers and the politics of education*. London: Routledge.

Goines, D. (2001). *Black girl lost*. Los Angeles: Holloway House.

Greene, B. (2007). In the beginning was the word . . . *Black issues book review* May/June, 20–23.

Griffin Jr., W. (1988). Follow the leader. In *Follow the Leader* [Audio recording]. Universal City, CA: UNI/MCA.

Halcón, J. (2001). Mainstream ideology and literacy instruction for Spanish-speaking children. In *The best for our children: Critical perspectives on literacy for Latino students*. New York: Teachers College Press.

Hanson, C. (Writer) (2002). *8 Mile*. B. Grazer, Hanson, C., & Iovine, J. (Producer). U.S.A.: Universal Studios and Dreamworks LLC.

Haynes, C., Crutcher, B J., Smith, C.W. (2002). Pimp juice. In *Nellyville* [Audio recording]. Los Angeles: Universal Music.

Heath, S. B. (1983). *Ways with words: Language, life, and work in communities and classrooms*. Cambridge: Cambridge University Press.

Hinton, S. E. (1997 [1967]). *The outsiders*. New Jersey: Prentice-Hall.

Hirsch, E. D. (1988). *Cultural literacy: What every American needs to know*. New York: Vintage.

Holman. K. (1997). English lesson. *Online NewsHour*. Accessed 4 Dec. at http://www.pbs.org/newshour/bb/congress/january97/ebonics_1–23.html.

hooks, b. (1994). *Teaching to transgress: Education as the practice of freedom*. New York: Vintage.

Hull, G., & Schultz, K. (Eds.). (2002). *School's out: Bridging out-of-school literacies with classroom practice*. New York: Teachers College Press.

Jackson, C. aka 50 Cent. (2003). P.I.M.P. In *Get rich or die tryin'* [Audio recording]. Santa Monica, CA: Interscope Records.

Jefferson, T., & Hall, S. (1990). *Resistance through rituals: Youth subcultures in post-war Britain*. London: Routledge.

Jones, K.; Adu, H. F.; Ditcham, M. R.; Winans, M. M. (2000). Single black female. In *Notorious K.I.M.* [Audio recording]. New York: Atlantic WEA Records.

Jones, N. aka Nas. (2002a). Made you look. In *God's son* [Audio recording]. New York: Columbia Records.

———. (2002b). I can. In *God's son* [Audio recording]. New York: Columbia Records.

———. (2002c). Warrior's song. In *God's son* [Audio recording]. New York: Columbia Records.

Kelley, R. (1994). *Race rebels: Culture, politics, and the Black working class*. New York: Free Press.

———. (1997). *Yo' mama's disFUNKtional!: Fighting the culture wars in urban America*. Boston: Beacon Press.

Kennedy, R. (2001). The triumph of robust tokenism. *The Atlantic monthly*, 287, 45–69.

Key, D. (1998). *Literacy shutdown: Stories of six American women*. Newark: National Reading Association.

Keyes, C. L. (2004). *Rap music and street consciousness*. Urbana, IL: University of Illinois Press.

Knobel, M. I'm not a pencil man: How one student challenges our notions of "failure" in schools. *Journal of adolescent & adult literacy* 44(5), 404–414.

Knobel, M. (1999). *Everyday literacies: Students, discourse, and social practice*. New York: Peter Lang.

Kweli, T. (1999). Know that (featuring Mos Def). On Mos Def, *Black on both sides* [Audio recording]. Los Angeles: Priority Records.

Lee, C. D. (1993). *Signifying as a scaffold for literary interpretation: The pedagogical implications of an African American discourse genre*. Urbana, IL: NCTE.

Light, A. (Ed.). (1999). *The Vibe history of hip hop*. New York: Three Rivers Press.

Mahiri, J. (1998). *Shooting for excellence: African American and youth culture in new century schools*. Urbana, IL: NCTE.

———— (Ed.). (2004). *What they don't learn in school: Literacy in the lives of urban youth*. New York: Peter Lang.

Mathers, M. aka Eminem. (1999). My name is. *The Slim Shady LP* [Audio recording]. Santa Monica: Interscope Records.

————. (2000). Superman. *The Marshall Mathers LP* [Audio recording]. Santa Monica: Interscope Records.

————. (2002). Lose yourself. *8 Mile* soundtrack. [Audio recording]. Santa Monica: Interscope Records.

McBride, D. (2002). *Impossible witnesses: Truth, abolitionism, and slave testimony*. New York: New York University Press.

McHenry, E., & Heath, S. B. (1994). The literate and the literary: African Americans as writers and readers 1830–1940. In E. Cushman, B. Kintgen, & M. Rose (Eds.), *Literacy: A critical sourcebook*. Boston: Bedford/St. Martin's.

McLaren, P. (2002). *Life in schools: An introduction to critical pedagogy in the foundations of education*. New Jersey: Pearson, Allyn, & Bacon.

McWhorter, J. (2003). How hip-hop holds Blacks back. *City journal*, 13(3).

Moje, E. (2000). "To be part of the story": The literacy practices of gangsta adolescents. *Teachers' College record*, 102(3), 651–659.

Morrell, E., & Duncan-Andrade, J. (2002). Toward a critical classroom discourse: Promoting academic literacy through engaging hip-hop culture with urban youth. *English journal*, 91(6), 67–85.

MTV2. (2003). *MTV2 Presents 22 Greatest MC's*. Air date 6 July.

Newkirk, T. (2002). *Misreading masculinity: Boys, literacy, and popular culture*. Portsmouth, NH: Heinemann.

Ogbu, J. (1991). Minority status and literacy in comparative perspective. In S. Graubard (Ed.), *Literacy: An overview by fourteen experts*. New York: Hill and Wang.

Olivo, W. (2001). Phat lines: Spelling conventions in rap music. *Written language & literacy* (4), 67–85.

Poertner, J. (2004). Shifting focus—From safety to permanence to well being. *"40 years of stewardship . . . where are we headed?" A report on the DCFS 40th Anniversary Symposium*. Chicago: Illinois Department of Children and Family Services.

Rodriguez, L. (1993). *Always running/La vida loca: Gang days in L.A.* New York: Touchstone.

Rodriguez, R. (1982). *Hunger of memory: The education of Richard Rodriguez*. New York: Bantam.

Rose, M. (1990). *Lives on the boundary*. New York: Penguin.

Rose, T. (1994). *Black noise: Rap music and Black culture in contemporary America*. Middletown, CT: Wesleyan U.P.

Rule, S. (1994, April 8). Generation rap. *New York Times*, 169–174.

Scott, J. (1990). *Domination and the arts of resistance: Hidden transcripts*. New Haven, CT: Yale U.P.

Shakur, T. (1991). Brenda's got a baby. In *2pocalypse now*. [Audio recording]. New York: Jive Records.

———. (1995). Dear Mama. On *Me against the world*. [Audio recording]. New York: Jive Records.

Sheridan, D.; Street, B.; & Bloome, D. (2000). *Writing ourselves: Mass observation and literacy practices*. New Jersey: Hampton Press.

Sim. (2003, March 28). Let's get some freestyles . . . [Msg. 170]. From http://www.aliciakeys.com:81/webx?14@844.F0ifa4IxcY0.9@.eea8f e5/39.

Sim & Jig. (2003, July 19). Let's get some freestyles . . . [Msg. 650 & 651]. From http://www.aliciakeys.com:81/webx?14@745.WedJabfbdGg. 32@.eea8fe5/1545.

Skorczewski, D. (2001, 4/12/04). Creating pleasurable experiences in the composition course (an interview with T. J. Johnson). *Voices from the field: An online conversation about the teaching of writing*. Retrieved June, from http://www.bedfordstmartins.com/voices/ index.html

Slim, I. (1987). *Pimp: The story of my life*. Los Angeles: Holloway House.

Smalls, C., aka Notorious B.I.G. (1994). Juicy. In *Ready to die* [Audio recording]. New York: Bad Boy Records.

Smith, D. aka Mos Def. (1999a). Fear not of man. On *Black on both sides* [Audio recording]. New York: Rawkus Records.

———. (2004). Close edge. *The new danger*. [Audio recording]. Santa Monica: Geffen Records.

———. (1999b). Love. In *Black on both sides*. [Audio recording]. New York: Rawkus Records.

———. (1999c). Hip Hop. In *Black on both sides*. [Audio recording]. New York: Rawkus Records.

Smith, M., & Wilhelm, J. (2002). *"Reading don't fix no Chevys": Literacy in the lives of young men*. Portsmouth, NH: Heinemann.

Smitherman, G. (1999). *Talkin that talk: Language, culture and education in African America*. London: Routledge.

Spivak, G. (1999). *A critique of post-colonial reason*. Cambridge, MA: Harvard U.P.

Street, B. (1995). *Social literacies: Critical approaches to literacy in development, ethnography and education*. London: Longman.

Sullivan, L. (1996). The demise of Black civil society: Once upon a time when we were colored meets the hip-hop generation. *Social policy*, 27, 6–10.

Tarpley, N. (Ed.). (1995). *Testimony: Young African-Americans on self-discovery and Black identity*. Boston: Beacon Press.

Toop, D. (2000). *Rap attack 3: African rap to global hip hop*. London: Serpent's Tail.

Valdes, G. (2001). *Learning and not learning English: Latino students in American schools*. New York: Teachers College Press.

Valdes, V., & Espino, J. (2003). *A closer look: Statistics for Latino majority schools in in the Chicago public schools*. Chicago: Aspira Inc. of Illinois/Chicagoland Latino Educational Research Institute (CLERI).

VH1. (2003). *VH1's one hundred greatest songs of the last 25 years* [Televised interview].

Villanueva, V. (1993). *Bootstraps: From an American academic of color*. Urbana, IL: NCTE.

Vygotsky, L. (1986). *Thought and language*. Cambridge, MA: MIT.

Walker, D. (1995[1829]). *David Walker's Appeal, In Four Articles: Together With A Preamble To The Coloured Citizens Of The World, But In Particular, And Very Expressly, To Those Of The United States Of America*. New York: Hill and Wang.

Weinstein, S. (2002). The writing on the wall: Attending to self-motivated student literacies. *English education*, 35(1), 21–45.

———. (2004). *"That ain't how I write": What teenagers know about literacy and learning*. Doctoral dissertation. University of Illinois at Chicago.

West, D. (2007). *Raising Kanye: Life lessons from the mother of a hip-hop superstar*. New York: Pocket Books.

West, K. (2004a). All falls down. On *College dropout* [Audio Recording]. New York: Roc-a-Fella.

———. (2004b). School spirit skit 1. On *College dropout* [Audio Recording]. New York: Roc-a-Fella.

———. (2004c). We don't care. On *College dropout* [Audio Recording]. New York: Roc-a-Fella.

Whitman, W. (1993). Song of myself. In *Leaves of grass* (25–76). New York: Barnes and Noble.

Williams, G. (2002). *The other side of the popular: Neoliberalism and subalternity in Latin America*. Durham: Duke U.P.

Williamson, L. (1996). *No disrespect*. New York: Vintage.

———. (2000). *The coldest winter ever*. New York: Pocket Books.

Willis, P. (1977). *Learning to labor: How working class kids get working class jobs*. New York: Columbia U.P.

Winnicott, D. W. (1971). *Playing and reality*. New York: Basic Books.

Index